# INNOVATIVE STUDENT RESIDENCES

New Directions in Sustainable Design

Avi Friedman
with John Wybor

images
Publishing

Published in Australia in 2016 by
The Images Publishing Group Pty Ltd
ABN 89 059 734 431
6 Bastow Place, Mulgrave, Victoria 3170, Australia
Tel: +61 3 9561 5544  Fax: +61 3 9561 4860
books@imagespublishing.com
www.imagespublishing.com

National Library of Australia Cataloguing-in-Publication entry:

| | |
|---|---|
| Title: | Innovative student residences : new directions in sustainable design / Avi Friedman. |
| ISBN: | 9781864705799 (hardback) |
| Notes: | Includes bibliographical references and index. |
| Subjects: | Architectural design. |
| | Student housing–Design. |
| | Architecture–Environmental aspects. |
| | Architecture, Modern–21st century. |

Other Creators/Contributors: Wybor, John, author.

| | |
|---|---|
| Dewey Number: | 371.871 |

Editor: Bethany Patch
Designer: Jason Phillips
Production Manager: Rod Gilbert
Senior Editor: Gina Tsahouras


Printed on 140gsm GoldEast Matt Art paper by Everbest Printing Co. Ltd., in Hong Kong/China


IMAGES has included on its website a page for special notices in relation to this and our other
publications. Please visit www.imagespublishing.com.

# Contents

# Preface

Students' residences were foreign to me when I began to study the subject. During my university years I shared a rented apartment with colleagues. Many aspects of my living accommodations were similar to students' housing, yet there was a marked difference between the two. I was not part of a large student community where social interactions take place and the university campus was not in our neighborhood.

That changed when Dr Deborah Buszard, the former dean of the faculty of agricultural and environmental sciences at McGill University in Montréal, Canada, called and asked me to look at a dilapidated student residence that was about to be demolished at the school's Macdonald Campus. It became evident to us that the building offered an opportunity to create a unique residential setting for students, while also supporting environmental causes.

In collaboration with the architectural firm L'OEUF, I have contributed to the design of the award-winning EcoResidence that saw the transformation of an existing structure.

It includes features such as improved thermal insulating values, reused old windows and doors, recycled brick, and the building of a new roof, among others. Alongside environmental improvements, we went on to establish social spaces both in the building and outside.

My design experience taught me that what makes student housing different from other types of lodging is the fact that the occupants–the students–are provided with a "home away from home" on the grounds of an academic institution. I recognized that it was likely to be the first time that these young students had left home and lived on their own, and needed to care for and interact with their place of living as an independent adult.

I also came to the realization that, to a degree, student residences can be regarded as an extension of classrooms. If suitably designed and introduced, student residences can become a teaching instrument about future housing that they will occupy once they have left university. For example, understanding energy-efficiency, and familiarization with

building materials and waste management, are subjects worth knowing about regardless of where one lives at a later stage of life.

In addition to knowledge about the building's physical aspects, the residences can become a backdrop for social learning. They can be incubators for new ideas when public spaces for their discussion and debate are set. If society regards its student population as its future brain trust, which all nations should do, developing opportunities for innovative or critical thinking outside the classroom can be part of the educational experience as well.

Graduating students in the 21st century are likely to face different challenges from those faced by preceding generations. Today's students need to obtain skills to function in a highly competitive job market, which from technological and economic perspectives, is progressing rapidly and changing often.

The tools that contemporary students now have at their disposal, whether technological or intellectual, are unparalleled. Therefore, students' residences need to be regarded as part of the new learning environment. The objective of future designs needs not only to conceive them as "lodging places," but as communities in the broad sense of the word, where a web of human relationships that support learning experiences will thrive. The transitory nature of student living needs to be countered by the sense of permanency that a good design offers. Simply put, students must feel that their room is their dwelling unit and part of a neighborhood.

Learning institutions are facing challenges as well. Perhaps chief among them is the need to be economically diligent. Many universities, primarily publically funded ones, have recently seen their budgets frozen or reduced. Doing "more with less" or even "less with less" has become the main contemporary paradigm and an influencing factor for most decision-making processes. The need to design accommodations that are functional and attractive, that cost less to build and operate, has become a priority and a guiding recipe for designers and administrators.

Attracting new students is also high on the list of many universities. Once buildings are built and professors hired, classrooms and dormitories need to be filled up. In an era of globalization, some schools set campuses away from their country of origin. Other institutions are actively recruiting students from around the globe. The traditional demographic and ethnic makeup of most institutions has changed. Student populations are more culturally diverse than in previous decades. Residents play an important role in not only attracting students, but also acting as a melting pot of sorts. A scan of many university websites demonstrates that the availability of well designed student housing and accessorized amenities have become an important drawing feature.

The urgent need to respond to local and global environmental challenges, as well as respect for regulations set by governments, is also evident. Scientific data points to dire natural consequences if action on climate change is not taken and new practices adopted. In 2007, the Intergovernmental Panel on

Climate Change (IPCC) published a report that addressed the role of humans in climate change. Among other observations, they found that global greenhouse gas (GHG) emissions resulting from human activities increased 70 percent from 1970 to 2004. The built environment in the developed world is known to be the third-largest contributor to GHG emissions, preceded by the industrial and transportation sectors. For example, in 2005 the residential sector of the Organization for Economic Cooperation and Development (OECD) countries contributed 21 percent of the total direct and indirect carbon dioxide emissions, totaling 23.1 gigatons.

Demand for energy is also growing rapidly. Between 1990 and 2005, electricity use in OECD countries increased by 54 percent. Although efforts are being put forward to increase efficiency in energy creation, delivery, and use, it has become abundantly clear that further steps will have to be taken to encourage design concepts that conserve natural resources and energy.

It is clear that "business as usual" cannot continue. Designers need to conceive of buildings that consume fewer natural resources during their construction and occupancy. Integrating new power-generating technologies, using new materials, elevating thermal insulation standards and encouraging students to consume less energy has become one of schools' uppermost priorities. A testimony to the change in design and construction practices of student housing is the recognition that many of the buildings featured in this book attained.

Another challenge, an indirect one, is the desire for universities to graduate well-rounded citizens. Setting up advanced curricula and research agendas, offering a healthy and active lifestyle, initiating extracurricular educational, and social activities, have started to occupy higher places on many schools' priority lists. Some universities are referring to it as "a student's experience." Living accommodations play a role in this endeavor. They are part of the "backstage" that supports these other priorities–to form a holistic approach to education.

I was invited to take part in such an approach in the design of the residences in Grizedale College at Lancaster University in the United Kingdom, a project featured in Chapter Four (see page 32). The project was designed by the firm GWP Architecture and led by architect John Wybor, to whom I acted as advisor.

Based on my research in the area of flexible and sustainable dwellings, the architectural model selected was a townhouse rather than the ubiquitous residential tower. The ground floor became "a social space" for the occupants of the rooms above. It was made to convey a domestic sense rather than look like a facility. On the environmental front, the buildings were constructed of renewable timber and included many ground-breaking features, such as solar water heating and pioneering mechanical heat-recovery ventilation. The project has proven to be affordable for both the developing firm and the university. It received an 'Excellent' rating of 71.4 percent in the United Kingdom's BREEAM award program.

This book addresses the issues that have been noted above and are likely to govern the design of future student housing. Each chapter begins with an essay that outlines the ideas that are related to the differing facets of student housing. The chapters also include several projects– of some of the most advanced student residences in the world–that are illustrated with text, images, and plans.

The first chapter further explains new realities and challenges that administrators and designers will face in the future. Chapter 2 looks at notions of flexibility in design, and the ability to create complexes made up of prefabricated components, such as shipping containers, which can be modified with ease when the need arises.

Chapter 3 considers integrative approaches to the design by examining how designers innovatively address a multitude of challenges, be they environmental, economic or functional, in a single design. Chapter 4 focuses on a signal subject–designs with low carbon footprints. Chapter 5 looks at student life in buildings and examines how designers address spaces for social interaction in a project. The chapter describes the use of common spaces and how they were conceived and utilized. The last chapter offers a historical chronology of student housing, dating back to the Middle Ages.

With each century, evolving societal challenges have led to the shifting and resetting of architectural priorities in many nations. The need to remodel old design ideas, and act upon them innovatively, has taken on an added importance in the 21st century. Student housing is part of this process. It is therefore hoped that this book will be of value to contemporary designers, university administrators and future students.

**Avi Friedman, 2016**

# Acknowledgments

Exploring innovative residential design ideas that respond to contemporary challenges– a result of economic, societal and environmental transformations–is the thrust of my teaching, research and practice. Over the years, many colleagues and students have contributed directly and indirectly to shaping these ideas. I would like to thank them all. In particular, I would like to recognize those who contributed to the creation of this monograph.

This book could not have been written without the contribution of my coauthor, architect John Wybor, director of GWP Architecture in Leeds, United Kingdom. My consultative role in the Lancaster University residences, and John's insights, were instrumental to my in-depth understanding of the subject. Two outstanding projects by his firm are featured here.

The contribution to the research and writing by a highly dedicated team is also much appreciated. Chloé DeBlois conducted the search for the projects and described them. Patricia Johnsson edited the project's description and added vital information. Zaphira Kalaitzakis helped with outstanding research and writing of each chapter's opening essay. She also drew the illustrations that accompany these chapters. Her contribution and dedication are truly remarkable. Appreciation is also due to Nyd Garavito-Bruhn, my assistant, who assembled and formatted the text and the illustrations.

Appreciation also goes to the faculty and staff of the McGill School of Architecture for creating an inspiring work environment. Finally, to my wife Sorel Friedman and children Paloma and Ben for their love and support.

# 01 Designing for New Realities

Contemporary student residences are designed with a multi-disciplinary approach, through a convergence of environmental challenges, economic circumstances and social consciousness. Many of the examples explored in this book seek to surpass the fundamental requirement of housing design, by innovatively combining higher education and living experiences. Often, this has been achieved by designing to suit a school's particular requirements and demographic—integrated with the surrounding environment—and by designing for a community of students.

Contemporary student housing is required to address multiple challenges. Governments commonly consider university graduates an asset to their country's prosperity. Offering student residences has become an incentive to attract potential students and to influence their selection of one school over another.

Globalization, advanced communication and ease of travel are raising rates of international enrolments in many nations (Fisher 2012). Student housing is a necessity for foreign and out-of-town students, and many students also choose to study away from home as part of their personal growth (Li 2011, Palmer 2012).

Another notable aspect of student housing is the large cohort of individuals reaching university age. Known as the "echo generation," the offspring of the baby-boomers are pursuing higher education in large numbers. The 18- to 24-year-old population cohort is expected to increase by approximately 4 million annually until the year 2020 in the United States alone (Zaransky 2006). Also in the United States, post-secondary full-time enrolments have increased by 1.3 million (or 12.4 percent) between the 2008/09 and 2011/12 academic years (Zaransky 2006, Johnson et al 2013).

Higher education is often considered mandatory in today's job market, leading to increased interest in university attendance (Zaransky 2006). More students are remaining in the education system for multiple or higher-level degrees, to become competitive in the job market. The Organization for Economic Cooperation and Development's

| Era | First student housing to 1900s | Post WWII | 1960s–70s | 1980s–90s | 2000–present |
|---|---|---|---|---|---|
| Attributes | • Aim to house students for learning<br><br>• Budget is limiting factor for quality/ design/ space | • Urgent, mass need for student housing<br><br>• Presence of veterans encourages schools to consider their needs | • Social revolution introduces social issues into student housing | • Need for technology in student housing<br><br>• Beginning of environmental awareness | • Well-rounded approach to design<br><br>• Needs of students at the forefront |
| Factors | • Shelter<br><br>• Study<br><br>• Economics | • Economics<br><br>• Shelter<br><br>• Study<br><br>• Student | • Economics<br><br>• Shelter<br><br>• Study<br><br>• Student<br><br>• Social | • Shelter<br><br>• Study<br><br>• Economics<br><br>• Student<br><br>• Social<br><br>• Technology<br><br>• Environment | • Student<br><br>• Shelter/study<br><br>• Economic/ social/ technology/ environment |

Factors influencing design of student housing by era

(OECD) data shows steady increases in member countries' tertiary-level educational achievements since the late 1990s. For example, in 2006, Canada had the highest percentage of tertiary-level attainment in its population—at 47 percent—an increase from 39.2 percent in 1999. Japan ranked second, with 40.5 percent—an increase from 31.8 percent in 1999 (OECD 2009). Both countries experienced an 8 percent increase in only seven years. Meanwhile, in the United States, student residences only house an average of 30 percent of the student population (Zaransky 2006). This shortage, and the expected rise in student population numbers, demonstrates a strong demand for housing in years to come.

In recent years, those pursuing higher education have been raised with an awareness of society's environmental challenges. As such, university housing has become a good educational vehicle for sustainable design practices.

Contemporary "green" building practices aim to reduce carbon footprints, both during construction and throughout a structure's life. According to the International Energy Agency (IEA), in most nations, buildings account for 40 percent of energy consumption, making them a prime target for energy efficiency (International Energy Agency n.d.). Therefore, it is imperative that the construction process and the final product are sustainable from the outset. Buildings can now generate energy from an alternative source, such as solar and geothermal power, and even feed the surplus energy back into the electricity grid (Vinnitskaya 2012). Proper siting of structures can also maximize sun exposure for passive solar gain (Friedman 2013, Shimm 2001).

As some projects in this chapter demonstrate, designers are also considering water efficiency.

Water usage can be minimized by installing appropriate fixtures, recycling greywater from showers and sinks, and harvesting rainwater (Friedman 2013). When possible, architects have incorporated green open spaces to allow for plant life, which adds to the quality of those spaces. Some housing units have been designed with prefabricated components for ease of construction and economy of scale and material. When combined, such methods can reduce operating costs while still exposing students to a sustainable lifestyle.

Sustainable design also involves the choice of materials. Advancements in manufacturing, and the depletion of raw materials, have led to innovations in the use of recycled or sustainable products (Friedman 2013). Project considerations can include analyses (such as cradle-to-cradle studies) to determine the energy required during manufacturing, and the transportation of materials and their environmental impact (Friedman 2012).

Design considerations can also be made to prolong the lifespan of student residences and to further enhance their sustainability. Some projects, for example, may offer more flexible spaces to accommodate growth and change. Inevitably, future generations of occupants will have different needs, and the transition is easier if projects have planned for easy alteration or expansion (Macintyre 2003).

Transportation is another factor, particularly with many urban schools now accommodating more sustainable modes of transportion, such as bicycles, by offering ample bicycle storage. Schools may choose to provide shuttle transportation between campuses or buildings, and they will work with cities to offer direct public transportion from the city center to the school.

Keeping within budget has always been a central aspect of providing education in the United States, especially since the 2008 global economic downturn. While enrolment is increasing, state funding to educational institutions is decreasing, creating harsh economic constraints (Zaransky 2006). According to the United States Center on Budget and Policy Priorities (CBPP), states spent about 28 percent less per student in higher education in 2013 than 2008 (Johnson et al 2013). These budgetary cuts mean that increasingly limited funds support a growing number of students, while there is less money to address the demand for student residences. Even though much of the existing student housing may be outdated, it might be more efficient, both economically and environmentally, to renovate rather than build anew (Shimm 2001).

While some institutions have available space for new housing on campus, others, especially urban institutions, may need to find a location off campus. In such cases, the project becomes part of an existing urban landscape, in addition to meeting the university's primary objectives. Consequently, the local economy is often positively affected by the presence of student housing (Macintyre 2003). Local property values may increase, yet local commerce may drop significantly over the summer months when students are away (Macintyre 2003).

Conversely, when properly planned and integrated in a mixed-use neighborhood, off-campus or urban campus housing can stimulate local economy (Macintyre 2003). Students create demand for amenities, restaurants and shops, support social establishments, and provide part-time employment. A diverse and dynamic student population can bring innovation and culture into a city through student-run activities. Local businesses can make use of student research and development, creating new technologies and start-up enterprises (Abel 2012). A student presence can also stimulate a neighborhood's renewal by guaranteeing a secure stream of income around university campuses and student housing (Abel 2012, Macintyre 2003). When well planned, student housing can become an integral asset and make a positive contribution to a community.

Contemporary student housing developments acknowledge the diverse needs of students. They aim to foster a learning environment, build lifelong relationships, and encourage school involvement (Peterkin 2013), while providing a smooth transition away from home. This transitional time is important because, for most students, university life is when they mature into adulthood and learn to care for themselves independently. Students are also expected to have up-to-date comprehensive amenities, such as private rooms with en suite bathrooms, laundry facilities, internet access, and social spaces.

In a university setting, it is expected that an integrated environment will accompany a diverse student population. Student housing should accommodate the variety of students that will use it, in terms of race, religion, disability, gender or sexual orientation (University of British Columbia n.d., University of Oregon n.d.). This establishes a precedent for equal opportunity and allows students to learn from their own diverse population. Many schools are now committed to providing such environments.

Students can benefit from a comfortable living environment, both emotionally and physically. Most schools offer health and wellness facilities, and security within living areas. Physical comforts are required both in private rooms and in the overall circulation of the complex. Academic leaders are shifting toward the concept of academic integration—the idea that learning is a continuous process that should not stop in the classroom (Peterkin 2013). Architecturally, this translates into multi-functional buildings that may contain living accommodations as well as classrooms, offices, and gathering spaces, to create a seamless learning experience that links academic and residential practices (Peterkin 2013).

Properly designed student residences consider all aspects of student life. They are multi-dimensional buildings that need to be creative and suitable for a school setting. They also need to integrate into surrounding environments—either an existing campus or an urban landscape. Lastly, they should serve every need and desire of a diverse student population, while contending with budgetary constraints and meeting sustainable specifications. This chapter illustrates these ideas with exemplary projects that successfully address new realities faced by today's administrators and students alike.

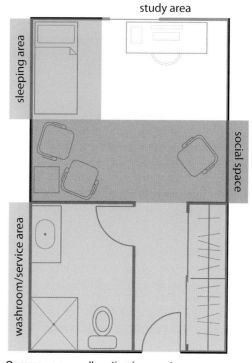

Common space allocation in a contemporary student room

# West Campus Student Housing Phase I

**Mahlum** // University of Washington, Seattle, United States

Completed in 2012, the West Campus Student Housing Phase I is an exemplary representation of a contemporary structure that includes student dwellings. Designed by Mahlum, this four-block mixed-use campus dwelling is a very important feature for the University of Washington. Situated in Seattle, the 688,800-square-foot (63,992-square-meter) development contains 1650 student beds throughout three mixed-use residence halls and an apartment residence—named Elm, Poplar, Alder and Cedar, respectively.

The publically accessible space within the West Campus Student Housing includes a 116-seat restaurant, 7000-square-foot (650-square-meter) grocery store, academic support center, and a health and wellness center. In addition to these features, this innovative student housing complex contains 132 parking spaces, available exclusively for residents of Cedar Apartments.

Two public open spaces are provided: a pocket park anchored by a heritage elm tree, and a courtyard allowing pedestrians

to cut through one residence hall at grade. Furthermore, every building benefits from a communal, secured terrace for its residents. More importantly, the landscaping and urban modifications made to the site and development plan are all aimed at improving the pedestrian experience.

Consequently, this project involved the narrowing of roadways, widening of sidewalks and planting of street trees. These hospitable additions, coupled with the 1650 student beds available, make this development quite impressive.

**Alder Hall (Ground level one)**

1   Conference center
2   Lower courtyard
3   Grocery service
4   Bike parking

0          100ft

**Alder Hall (Residential level three)**

1 Residential roof terrace
2 Floor lounges
3 Residential rooms
  (108 beds per floor)

**Poplar Hall (Ground level two)**

4 Residential commons
5 Retail spaces
6 Studio apartments
7 Bike parking
8 Accessible parking
9 Service

**Elm Hall (Ground level two)**

10 Elm plaza
11 Restaurant
12 Residential commons
13 Studio apartments
14 Service
15 Accessible parking

**Cedar Apartments (Ground level one)**

16 Residential commons
17 Parking (71 stalls)
18 Service

**Alder Hall (Ground level two)**

1 Grocery store
2 Café
3 Courtyard
4 Residential commons
5 Residential rooms (33 beds)
6 Alder Hall bus stop

**Poplar Hall (Ground level one)**

7 Advisory suite
8 Academic resource center
9 Central custodial offices

**Elm Hall (Ground level one)**

10 Elm plaza
11 Health & wellness center
12 Bike parking
13 Elm Hall bus stop

0    100ft

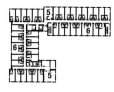

**Alder Hall (Residential levels five–seven)**
1   Floor lounge
2   Residential rooms (108 beds per floor)

**Poplar Hall (Residential levels four–seven)**
3   Floor lounge
4   Residential rooms (53 beds per floor)

**Elm Hall (Residence levels four–seven)**
5   Floor lounge
6   Residential rooms (85 beds per floor)

**Cedar Apartments (Residential levels three–seven)**
7   Residential roof terrace (Level 3)
8   Studio, two- & four-bedroom apartments

**Alder Hall (Residential level four)**
1   Floor lounge
2   Residential rooms (108 beds per floor)

**Poplar Hall (Residential level three)**
3   Residential roof terrace
4   Floor lounge
5   Residential rooms (53 beds per floor)

**Elm Hall (Residence level three)**
6   Residential roof terrace
7   Floor lounge
8   Residential rooms (85 beds per floor)

**Cedar Apartments (Residential level two)**
9   Two- & four-bedroom townhomes
10  Parking (54 stalls)
11  Bike parking

# West Village (first phase)

**Studio E Architects** // University of California, Davis, United States

In 2011, the first phase of the University of California (UC) Davis West Village opened in the Upper Central Valley. The West Village is an example of large-scale university planning. The site is 6,011,320 square feet (558,470 square meters), half of which remains untouched as the future site of single-family homes. The project will eventually accommodate 3000 students and 44,000 square feet (4089 square meters) of commercial space in this public–private partnership development.

The buildings vary in color, in warm shades of orange, red and yellow, but are all topped by a "saw-toothed roof" design. The roofs provide deep overhangs on the southern façades for shade and protection from the hot Californian sun, while allowing the interior to warm naturally in winter. The southern and western façades are also ventilated with vertical corrugated metal, protecting the buildings from heat gain.

The project's stated objective was to utilize advanced energy-saving methods and technologies in order to achieve a net-zero energy consumption. For instance, superior insulation, photovoltaic panels, shading devices and reflective roofs were integrated throughout the buildings. Every roof is tilted towards a southern orientation and is designed to support a maximum number of photovoltaic panels. In addition to these sustainable building methods, students can control aspects of the building's energy consumption with their smart phones in each of the 662 apartments. They can turn off lights and plugs, and see their real time consumption, through a sophisticated, energy-monitoring software. The appliances and fixtures used are also energy-efficient, further reducing energy use.

As well as sustainability, the design focused on creating a space to promote interaction between students. Gathering areas are available and the buildings are arranged to create situations where people can meet and enjoy the outdoors. The proximity of the apartments to mixed-use buildings, recreation fields, and the community college, all contribute to the social interactions on campus. In these residences, student life is both ecological and engaging, taking advantage of its Californian setting in every sense.

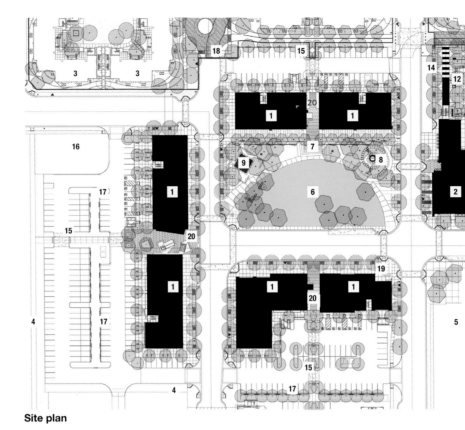

**Site plan**

1  Mixed-use
2  Recreational buildings
3  Student apartments
4  Future faculty/staff housing
5  Community facility
6  Village green
7  Bandshell
8  Bioswale garden
9  Fountain
10 Pool
11 Volleyball court
12 Barbeque area
13 Terrace garden
14 Mail
15 Pedestrian connection
16 Future community center site
17 Bioswale
18 Sunrise walk
19 Dining terrace
20 Paseo

DESIGNING FOR NEW REALITIES

# Smarties, Uithof

**Architectenbureau Marlies Rohmer** // Utrecht University, Utrecht, the Netherlands

The project's objective was to relieve the student housing shortage at Utrecht University in the city of Utrecht, the Netherlands. The result is the freestanding student accommodation building known as Smarties, which consists of a solid mass with a cantilevered portion of 66 feet (20 meters) and houses 380 independent rooms.

The supporting structure is made of four slabs of concrete painted bright green, which enhances and complements the building's natural surroundings. The building mass rests on the slabs, which are penetrated by a longitudinal corridor containing the students' units, with a total area of 200,209 square feet (18,600 square meters).

The building's façade is made of a grid of multi-colored aluminum panels, which represent the diversity of international students that come to study at the university. Meanwhile, the green slabs accentuate the entrance to create a gathering place for students. On one of the overhanging end façades, a swing bench is suspended to create a space for leisure and interaction.

The interior's design also aims to promote interaction between students. A roof terrace, party rooms, and niches along corridors and staircases, encourage and support social connections. The building's height, 164 feet (50 meters), creates a welcome contrast between the rural surroundings and the other buildings. The south side of the structure faces Heidelberglaan, a main access route with a bus stop. The Smarties residence is united, both inside and out, by its emphasis on creating contact between students. It is an excellent example of a residence offering more to a student's everyday life than just a place to sleep.

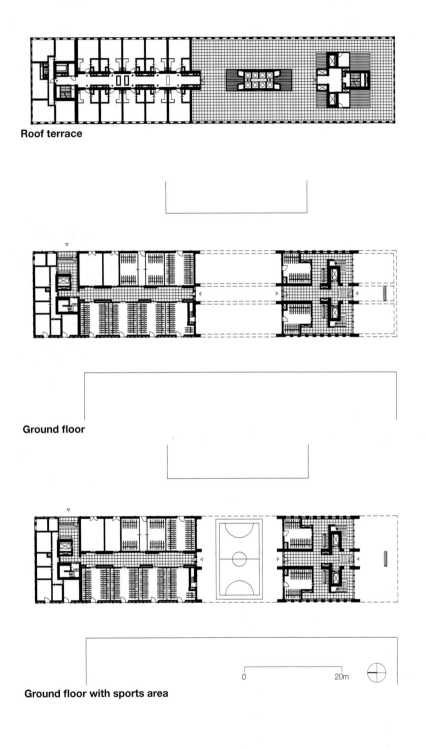

Roof terrace

Ground floor

Ground floor with sports area

0          20m

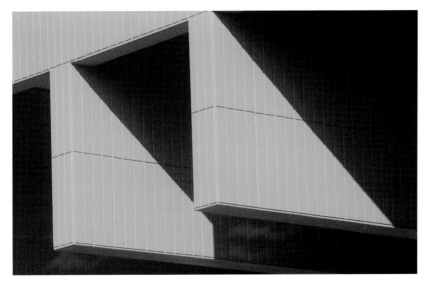

# Student Village

**Hawkins\Brown** // Royal Veterinary College, Potters Bar, United Kingdom

The Royal Veterinary College commissioned London architects Hawkins\Brown to design new student housing at the college's Hawkshead campus. The design is especially sensitive to the local rural environment, while also emphasizing the needs of its occupants.

The project is organized as a series of three- and four-story pavilions, linked by a lightweight aluminum-clad lift and stair core. Each pavilion contains six-bedroom modules that are grouped around a shared kitchen and a meeting area, with a total of 190 en suite rooms. A larger building houses the community meeting area and the dining hall, occupying a total area of 69,750 square feet (6480 square meters).

For the choice of exterior cladding, the architects acknowledged the local rural environment of Hertfordshire by using western red cedar timber and Bronsgroen bricks. These materials are affordable, sustainable and require a low level of maintenance. The aluminum siding of the circulation cores was conceived and built in collaboration with the artist Nicky Hirst. It is

perforated with full- and half-moon shapes to protect students from the weather.

The project was rated BREEAM 'Very Good', a sustainability rating for "green" buildings in the United Kingdom. The Royal Veterinary College achieved this recognition by introducing systems such as bicycle parking, water and

energy management, solar hot water and greywater recycling, and through the use of sustainable materials such as timber.

These environmental practices work in conjunction with the new accommodations, restaurant and conference rooms to provide students with unique amenities.

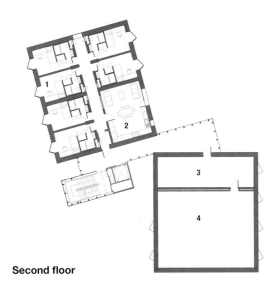

**Second floor**

**First floor**

**Ground floor**

1  Typical student accommodations
2  Typical living/kitchen area
3  Plant room
4  External plant area

0        5m

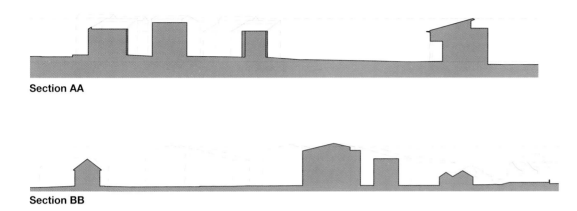

Section AA

Section BB

# Student Apartments in the Olympic Village

**Werner Wirsing and bogevischs buero** // Studentenwerk München, Munich, Germany

In 1972, architect Werner Wirsing designed the Olympic Village in Munich, and the women's section of the athletes' village has since served as student housing. Originally, the complex comprised an arrangement of 800 identical concrete units. Each unit occupied an area of 258 square feet (24 square meters) and comprised a kitchen, bathroom, roof terrace and gallery.

Years later, these units were in dire need of renovation due to deteriorating sanitation, waterproofing and insulation conditions. Since refurbishment costs were high, the client, Studentenwerk München (Munich's student union in charge of accommodations), decided to rebuild them with a focus on historic preservation. Werner Wirsing collaborated with the firm bogevischs buero to design

1052 student accommodations that would be based on the old cube houses, while keeping and renovating just 12 of the original units. The new apartments were closely based on the size and proportion of the original ones. However, the complex maximized its space more efficiently to provide 252 extra apartments, in the same 430,556 square feet (40,000 square meters) of area.

Today, students are allowed to paint the concrete façade of their unit in their chosen color. Each unit contains a terrace with external access. Students can find pubs, coffee shops and discos nearby. The architects have successfully renewed the Olympic Village spirit by preserving its architectural heritage, while maintaining a sense of individual expression within a community.

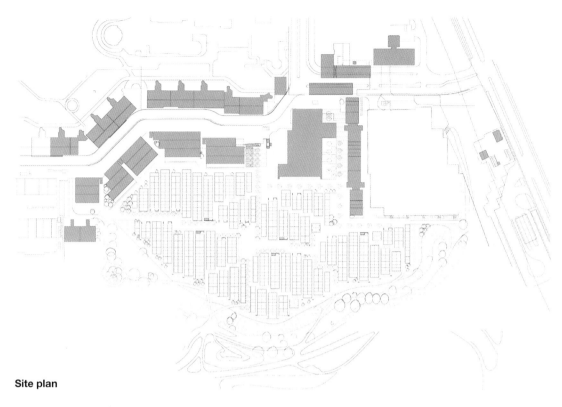

**Site plan**

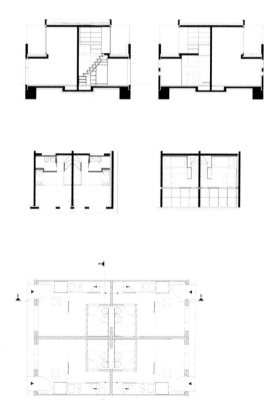

**Typical rooms**

# Newington Green Student Housing

**Haworth Tompkins Architects** // University of London, London, United Kingdom

The goal of this project was to revitalize the disadvantaged neighborhood of Newington Green in London, by introducing new and renovated residences for students of the University of London. In addition, the architects wanted to unite traditional student housing with the residential character of the surrounding area.

The project contains two distinct elements: the renovated China Inland Mission building and four new student accommodation blocks, located at the back of the site. The China Inland Mission building has been converted to a student hostel, office space, and retail units, which form the gateway to the site. Together, the five student residences occupy an area of 57,307 square feet (5324 square meters).

In total, 213 new student residences were made available in the Newington Green Conservation Area. The residences are mainly single en suite rooms, 8 by 13 feet (2.5 by 4 meters). The newly constructed blocks are oriented north–south to maximize views and let in sunlight. Each new block consists of two white pavilions paired around an open staircase, covered in vertical larch slat cladding.

The large numbers of mature trees that exist on the site offer the impression of a secret garden in the heart of the city. The garden becomes a pathway that connects the new blocks of the project to the China Inland Mission building. Students can find privacy in their single rooms, while also engaging with each other in the urban garden, which acts as a sanctuary in a fast-paced city.

**Long section**

0    10m

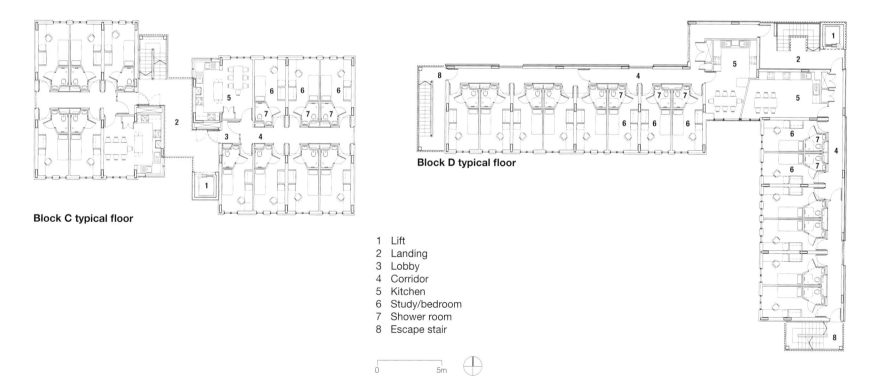

**Block C typical floor**

**Block D typical floor**

1 Lift
2 Landing
3 Lobby
4 Corridor
5 Kitchen
6 Study/bedroom
7 Shower room
8 Escape stair

0            5m

# Student Housing Duwo

**Mecanoo Architecten** // Delft University of Technology, Delft, the Netherlands

The number of students enrolled at the Delft University of Technology has increased in recent years, resulting in a growing demand for student housing. The university therefore decided to expand its student accommodations by 1700 units. However, as conventional construction of these units was projected to take several years, the architectural firm Mecanoo was asked to develop a concept for rapid construction that could address the university's immediate needs. The project consists of three blocks, six stories tall, which house a total of 186 students in an area of 102,257 square feet (9500 square meters). Each living unit has its own kitchen and bathroom.

Mecanoo was given one year to oversee the project from initial design to occupancy. A modular construction system was selected, and each of the three blocks was prefabricated and followed an identical design. The blocks' cores are made of concrete, and include a staircase and an elevator, while steel-frame structures support the housing units. Entrances are located on the first floor where common facilities, such as bicycle parking and storage space, can be found.

On each block, three of the façades are clad in dark masonry, while the fourth is painted green. A tubular frame has been specifically installed to encourage climbing plants to grow along this façade in the warmer months. Pastures and greenery surround the buildings, while large windows offer attractive views. The windows are staggered at different heights, including gaps, which create unique interior and exterior effects. In fact, every room has a window at a different spot. Mecanoo provided careful detailing in these rapidly built structures, and responded to an immediate need with an enduring design.

**Section**

STUDENT HOUSING DUWO

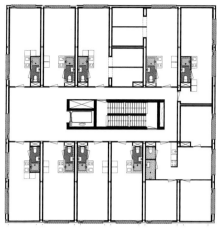

**Second floor**

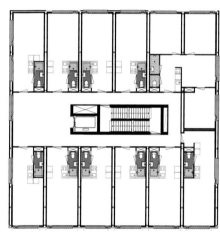

**First floor**

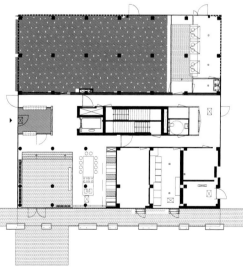

**Ground floor**

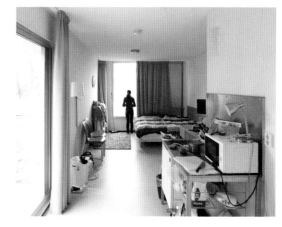

# 02 Flexibility in Student Housing

Ongoing changes are a reality in today's built environment. Quick overturn, new technologies, and a consumption-driven economy, have shortened the expected life cycles of everyday products and buildings. However, with the rise of sustainable practices and a "cartel-to-cartel" approach to planning, designing for flexibility can influence the longevity and functionality of a building. Adaptability also allows a building to reflect shifts in demographic, economic, technological and environmental requirements.

For student housing, decisions made during the design and construction process can affect the long-term needs of a school. Flexibility may encompass macro changes that impact the entire building, including adding or removing space, or repurposing the building's function. It can also foster changes within rooms, spatial arrangements or upgrades to technology. Designing for change ensures a longer lifespan for the building and better accommodations for the changing needs of students. This chapter looks at flexible design in student residences and techniques used for its application.

Data shows that in the coming decades university enrollments will increase, along with demand for student housing in most nations. However, it is difficult to accurately predict

future use. Societal changes will determine the overall space needed for a school's housing. Yet, when properly conceived, flexible design can serve both schools and students. Spaces intended for change can include common areas, study spaces or multi-purpose rooms. Flexible design can arrange to fit a variety of students' needs through single rooms, more privacy in shared rooms, or by having apartment-style suites. Some schools attract graduate students by offering larger units for young families. When students' needs are adequately met, they will continue to use those accommodations, rather than rent their own apartments away from campus. For student housing to remain competitive, schools must offer unique environments to include a sense of community and a diverse learning setting. Since these needs may transform, student housing should change with them to remain relevant and to draw new occupants.

Universities have evolved over centuries and are expected to be pillars of society for years to come. Recent economic conditions have left schools with less public funding and increasingly tight budgets. Well designed student housing should have longevity to reduce a school's costs. While trying to maintain quality, a flexible

design approach could help reduce alteration costs, as there is often little money to waste. When a building is designed for easy expansion or reuse, a school can avoid future requirements to add new buildings. Designing to facilitate maintenance can also reduce the costs of future repairs. With increasing international competition for students, up-to-date living accommodations are more attractive to them. Attaining full occupancy then ensures continued revenue streams for the school.

As construction evolves, an area that requires constant adjustment is technology. For student housing, there are two main types of technologies to consider—those that involve operation and those that are necessary in daily student life. The first includes "green" technology, such as plumbing, electrical, heating and ventilation systems, and thermal insulation upgrade. These technologies are very likely to advance. Although some practices may be at the forefront today, over time they will certainly change to become more efficient. The second is part of the learning experience. Students rely heavily on wireless computers and the internet for learning, making the experience more mobile, visual, interactive and connected (JISC 2006). This needs to be reflected in the spaces they occupy, affecting the size and locations of study areas, wi-fi accessibility, and internet security (JISC 2006). Taking these technologies into consideration and allowing for their upgrade will better ensure their successful integration into the learning environment in the years ahead.

A significant part of sustainable design is the impact of a building on the environment. A flexible design approach minimizes construction waste, for instance, but also prolongs the life of a building. Through early planning for space reconfiguration, the building can serve its function for longer. By considering these inevitable design changes, it may imply that there will also be future ecological benefits as an effect of including flexibility in the design.

A technique that may be employed in the design process, to achieve flexibility, is the use of industrialized components. Modular construction can be more cost- and time-effective than onsite construction. It can also be made to accommodate vertical or horizontal additions. Modular construction occurs in 60 to 90 percent of an offsite-controlled environment (Hardiman 2011). The modules can be built as complete housing units or as sections only (Common Ground 2013). Once completed, the elements are then trasnported to the site and assembled. They can be customized to include fixtures, plumbing, finishes, fireproofing and a variety of materials with designs to accommodate any style or need (Hardiman 2011).

Modular construction allows for time efficiencies that work well for schools, completing projects 30 to 50 percent faster than traditional site construction, and reducing high-risk onsite work. If construction takes place during the summer when the school is vacated, it minimizes disruptions once the school year starts. Since most construction takes place in a factory setting, there are also environmental benefits to modular

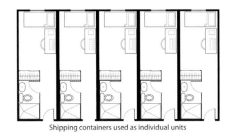
Shipping containers used as individual units

Modular units joined to make apartment-style housing

**Modular construction types in student residences**

construction. Manufacturers, for example, can arrange for energy savings and less material waste during the process (Hardiman 2011).

However, there are some drawbacks to this process that are worth considering. For instance, the manufacturers need to supply quality products that fit the school's vision. Modular units can create a variety of sizes and shapes for buildings, yet there are limitations in adapting to irregular site conditions, such as a hill (Cardenas and Domenech 2005), that may require more onsite construction. External factors can also influence the decision to use this type of construction. A school or a city may prefer to employ local workers for construction, rather than using external sources, to enhance economic benefits. However, it is clear that the benefits that modular construction offers to schools are undeniable. The very nature of modular building suits the uniform needs of this kind of project (Cardenas and Domenech 2005).

Another method that has become popular in the construction of student residences is the use of shipping containers. Similar to modular construction, containers can be stacked and arranged to form a complex. Containers offer some of the same benefits as modular construction—faster construction time, flexibility in size and shape, and the ability to make later additions. However, it is a much less cost-efficient process. There are hidden expenses in converting containers into livable units fitted with doors and windows, plumbing and insulation. It might also seem like an environmentally friendly option to use recycled containers for the units, but most large-scale projects have resorted to buying new containers due to the high cost of refurbishing used ones (Common Ground 2013). This does provide another option for creating units within a student housing complex, yet a school may choose this method for its novelty rather than its practicality.

If the intention is to plan for future changes to the building, whether by addition or subtraction, the chosen framework and structure should support those changes. The methods of using modular or container units are excellent ways to ensure that units can be successfully added down the track. If, from the outset, vertical additions are a foreseeable option, the design can include a proper foundation and supports to minimize future renovation costs. If space permits, horizontal expansion is simpler, especially when existing corridors can be extended. The support structures, and dimensioning of the internal spaces, can increase the capability for future alterations (Schneider and Till 2007). This is restricted with shipping container units, because they are most commonly used as individual units. Modular units can more easily be designed for flexible interior programs.

Flexibility in student housing can result from interior design choices and space arrangements. Movable interior partitions may be used. These are easily built walls that offer the possibility to modify room plans. Rooms can then be rearranged to suit changing internal demands. For instance, small rooms can be joined together to form larger rooms that accommodate more students. The use of large multi-purpose rooms in housing complexes allow for future opportunities to rearrange space. These areas are often used as common gathering spaces or study areas. By modifying interior partitions, these spaces can grow or shrink in size according to changing needs. For instance, they can become classrooms or offices, offering flexible options for the school.

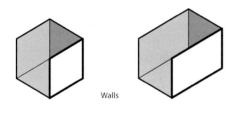

Walls

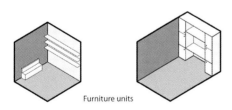

Furniture units

**Prefabricated components may include walls and furniture**

Interior arrangements can also offer flexible functions for a student housing complex. Depending on the room setup, schools can adapt accommodations to be used as hotels or rental apartments in the summer (McGill

University n.d.). To complement their student housing, many schools offer apartments for their students, especially for mature graduate students with families who may prefer to live more independently. These units can then be re-sold or rented to the public. For most other housing units, the arrangement often depends on the services provided by the school and the number of students they need to accommodate. If the school can supply a cafeteria, then they can arrange smaller rooms without kitchens for larger numbers of students. This facility can be converted for use as a hotel. Some schools can only supply shared kitchens and washrooms to accompany student rooms. If the number of students is smaller, then the school can arrange for more independent living conditions, such as apartment-style accommodations, which may be sold or rented. A school's location is relevant to these choices, as it will affect the amenities available to students if they are to live more independently. Location also becomes a factor in the building's reuse, if the function can be changed. Metropolitan schools may have more opportunities to rent units as apartments or to use their housing as hotels during the summer.

If student housing managers have the option to change the purpose of the accommodation to apartments or a hotel, at a later stage, the circulation of the space should remain functional. Factors that affect circulation include entrances, lobbies, hallways, elevators and stairs. These should be considered if the intention for the building is to change. They are also important for how the students will use the space. As many schools leave open spaces for gathering and socializing, the transitions from these public spaces to private spaces should be well intentioned and comfortable for students.

They can also transition well for multi-unit housing (Schneider and Till 2007). If present and future circulation patterns are considered in a flexible design, the transition into different uses for the space will be more successful.

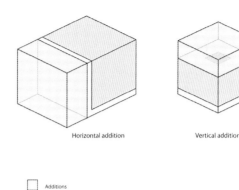

Horizontal addition        Vertical addition

Additions

Circulation

Student accomodations

**Expansion in student housing can be made easier if properly designed**

Flexible design in student housing is highly useful for higher education institutions. Often there are demands for well-rounded, smarter designs in architecture. Flexibility acknowledges and plans for the inevitable, changing needs of the student population, the economic and environmental conditions faced, and the rapidly changing reliance on technologies. These acknowledgments make designing for flexibility intrinsically sustainable on multiple levels. Through proper planning and function, it is a way to ensure all available space is used. The examples that follow will show some of the techniques and benefits of flexible design.

# Zuiderzeeweg

**Fact Architects** // De Key Corporation, Amsterdam, the Netherlands

Zuiderzeeweg is a temporary, flexible, student housing complex in Amsterdam. The building was designed to be movable, in order to follow the student housing demands of the social housing corporation De Key. This corporation builds, manages and rents out rooms to students in Dutch universities.

The project includes a number of sustainable features and was conceived to maintain the same functions when moved to another location. The six five-story-block buildings comprise a total of 335 student units in 133,419 square feet (12,395 square meters). The units are high quality, prefabricated modules with an area of 334 square feet (31 square meters), each including a balcony, windows, a floor-heating system and a bathroom. When the manufacture of the units was completed, they were transported to the temporary site and stacked on top of each other to form six buildings.

The buildings enclose a large courtyard with lawns and a sports field. Bike parking is also available along the adjacent road, while a train stop nearby provides easy access to public transportation. Concrete blocks, used as outdoor seating, were installed near the entrance.

The architects designed a durable façade of dark wood and distinctive orange lettering to mark the buildings' entrances. This choice of contrasting materials gives the complex a permanent and durable feel. Private balconies to each unit are also a dominant characteristic of the façade. Zuiderzeeweg provides students with a sustainable lifestyle amid any landscape, while also offering privacy and accessibility.

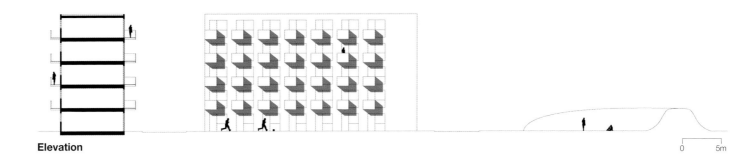

**Elevation**

0    5m

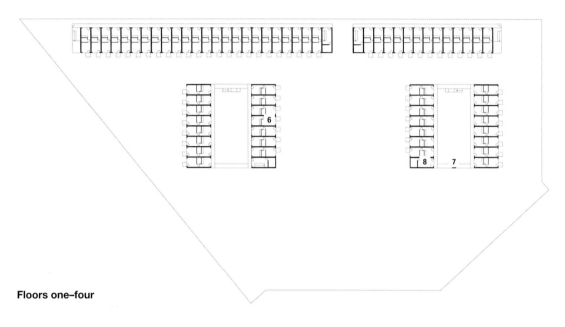

**Floors one–four**

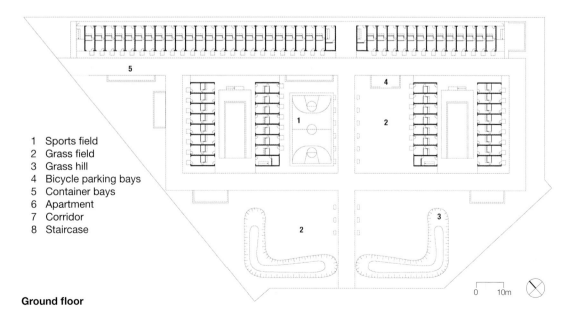

1 Sports field
2 Grass field
3 Grass hill
4 Bicycle parking bays
5 Container bays
6 Apartment
7 Corridor
8 Staircase

0    10m

**Ground floor**

# Student Housing

**H Arquitectes and dataAE** // Universitat Politècnicade Catalunya, Sant Cugat del Vallès, Spain

The new student housing at the Polytechnic University of Catalonia is located near the School of Architecture, but it is not limited to architecture students. The project attempts to establish a balance between old and new construction, and is composed of two-story-tall blocks placed parallel to each other and separated by a central atrium.

The building comprises 57 prefabricated units and occupies 25,833 square feet (2400 square meters). This industrialized building process has various advantages, such as time saving techniques, quality control and waste reduction. In fact, the project saved 50 percent of embedded energy associated with construction materials. The exterior of the building was clad with galvanized steel, while a polycarbonate roof was built above the central terrace. This space can be used as an assembly area for the students.

It also helps create natural ventilation, which reduces energy consumption and the need for mechanical cooling.

Every module is made of a precast concrete cube, with no interior partitions, and includes fixtures such as a kitchenette and a washroom. The fixtures are installed using dry-build methods for the purpose of creating modules that can easily be dismantled, reused or recycled, depending on the changing needs of the university. The adaptability of the units is echoed in the interior of the apartments. The module was left unpainted, as a flexible space where students can personalize the design of their own unit, which is especially appealing to the architecture students who occupy the building.

The project is a successful example of a structure that will be viable for years to come, offering many possibilities of reconfiguration to both the students and the university.

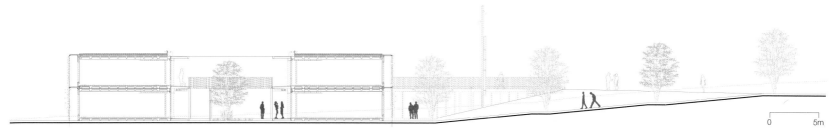

**Section**

0    5m

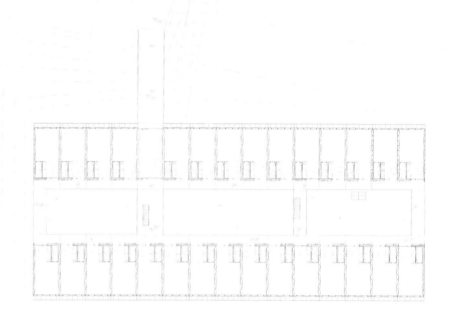

**First floor**

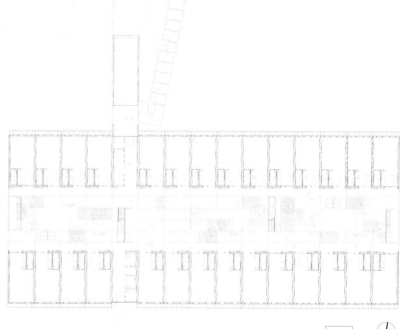

**Ground floor**

0  5m

# Keetwonen (Amsterdam Student Housing)

**Tempohousing Global** // De Key Corporation, Amsterdam, the Netherlands

Keetwonen is the biggest container city in the world. In fact, this residence is the second-most popular among students in Amsterdam, according to the De Key Corporation who manages it. Since these temporary units are so popular, their relocation has been postponed until 2016. The site includes a total of 1000 units arranged in blocks, occupying 355,209 square feet (33,000 square meters). A café, supermarket, office spaces and a sports area are also available for students.

The blocks of units are arranged linearly— a series of rectangular prisms of varying sizes—reminiscent of the containers from which they are composed. Working with containers offers many advantages. They are low cost, mobile, allow for rapid assembly, and contain a kitchen, sleeping area, study space and a balcony. The units offer considerably private space for their low cost, a major benefit of the Keetwonen project. Contrary to common perception, the containers are spacious, quiet, and energy-efficient. Each unit also contains a large window for views and natural light.

Units are also equipped with an automated multi-speed ventilation system, and an audio phone system for visitors at the main door. An enclosed area was also created for bicycle parking. Tempohousing Global has designed a space that appeals to students by including private amenities as well as areas for social interactions—all at an affordable price.

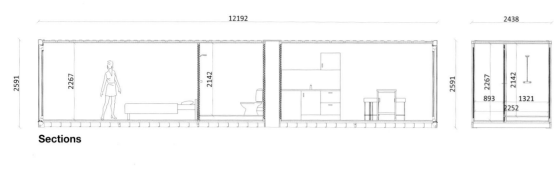

**Sections**

**Floor plan**

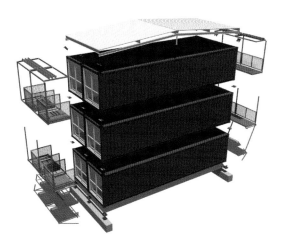

# Signalhuset

**NOBEL arkitekter** // Ørestad, Denmark

The Signalhuset is located in the City of Ørestad, near Copenhagen. The 10-story building on Arne Jacobsens Street faces a canal. It contains 288 student units, elevated on concrete legs that can be amalgamated to form 72 single-family dwellings on a site measuring 26,372 square feet (2450 square meters).

The façade stands out—with the combination of vibrant colors applied to each unit and the external, transparent screens of galvanized, stretched-metal frames on each balcony. The choice of materials, which includes glass, steel and stone, has a practical function. It filters out the sunlight throughout the housing units. As a visitor to the building, its appearance changes when viewed from different directions due to its lively façade.

The design concept used in this project is called the "four-in-one" principle because four student accommodations can be easily transformed into one family apartment. The four student units are organized around two shared bathrooms, a kitchen and a small common area, offering each student 108 square feet (10 square meters) of private space and 161 square feet (15 square meters) of shared space. The adaptability of this space gives the building a dual function—it can accommodate students or families depending on the university's needs.

The elevated structure invites both the students and the public to walk around the open ground level area. A café and common areas occupy the courtyard in this space. The Signalhuset serves more than just its current student residents. It provides Ørestad with a lively, adaptable structure that will accomodate the community for years to come.

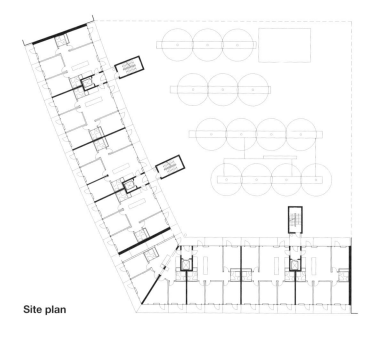

Site plan

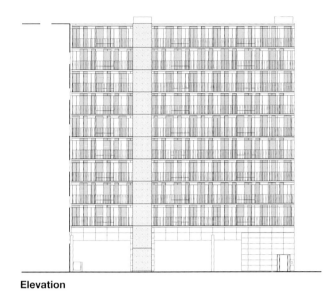

**Elevation**

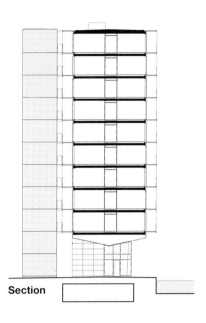

**Section**

# La Résidence Pour Étudiants du Havre en Containers Maritimes

**Charlotte Cattani and Alberto Cattani Architectes** // CROUS Rouen Haute Normandie, Le Havre, France

These architects designed a student housing project that comprises 100 apartments made from recycled shipping containers. By leaving areas between the units to form balconies, walkways and patios, the living spaces feel spacious and open. To provide the building with further lightness and transparency, an exposed metal frame was used to act as the structural support for the containers.

The units measure 258 square feet (24 square meters) each, and include a bathroom, kitchen, sleeping area, and workspace. The structure is four stories tall, but the main level is raised aboveground to give occupants privacy from passersby. By raising the first floor, a bicycle storage space was created on that additional level.

Each unit overlooks an indoor garden and is fenestrated at both ends by glass walls, which let in natural light. To reduce noise transmission, the sidewalls that are between apartment or facing the exterior are sound-insulated, with reinforced concrete firewalls and rubber that is 16 inches (40 centimeters) wide. The building's exterior façade—a mix of black steel and metallic gray containers—contrasts heavily with the interior, painted in white with wooden furniture.

This dichotomy between the façade and the interior allows the project to complement its industrial surroundings, while providing students with a serene and welcoming atmosphere.

LA RÉSIDENCE POUR ÉTUDIANTS DU HAVRE EN CONTAINERS MARITIMES

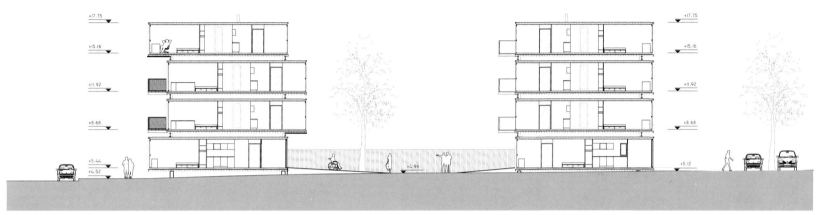

**Section**

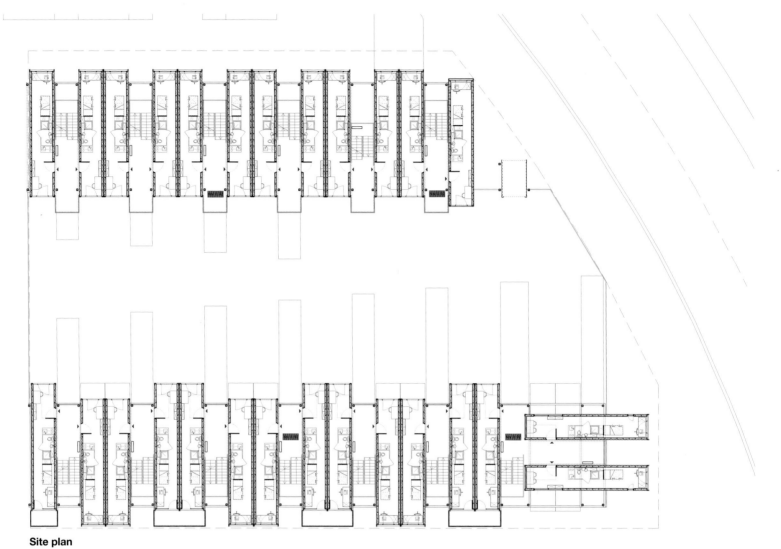

**Site plan**

# Qubic

**Studioninedots** // De Key Corporation, Amsterdam, the Netherlands

Qubic comprises temporary student accommodations in the former dockland area of Amsterdam's Houthaven neighborhood. Some 1000 students are housed in 715 former shipping containers. In addition to the students' housing units, a ship has also been converted into student rooms, studios for artists, restaurants, and bars.

The project's design and construction were rapid and lasted only 12 months. Accommodations consist of stacked, 30- by 10-foot (9- by 3-meter) containers placed between two prefabricated, structural planes. This method has various benefits: it ensures a robust and reusable structure, costs are kept to a minimum, and elevated verandas are formed. The housing units can be accessed via long double-loaded corridors, which are well lit and ventilated, due to intentional gaps where containers have not been included in the structure.

The buildings' façades are composed of molded plastic panels with window openings. In addition, colored Plexiglass was added to create a lively and vibrant space. The housing was positioned around three open areas that serve as public gathering places—each block occupying an area of 269,098 square feet (25,000 square meters). This planning concept reinforced the objective to create a "village-like" atmosphere. Despite the impermanence of the student housing project, the buildings have succeeded in appearing stable and being a fixture of the landscape. The units have helped unify the area, which had previously been a random grouping of freestanding buildings.

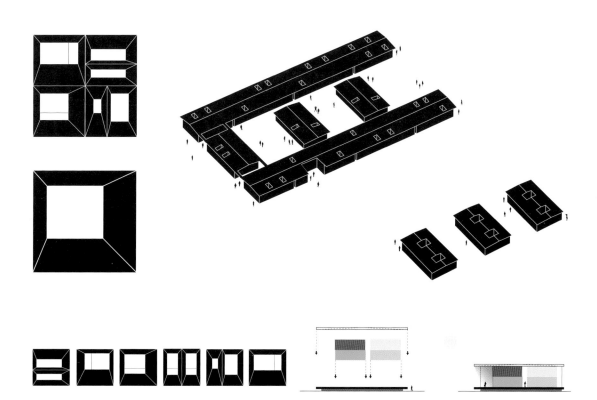

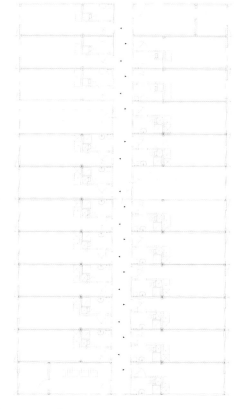

**Floor plan**

# 03 Integrative Approaches to Design

Contemporary student housing must meet a range of new requirements—a task that alters the traditional design process. In recent times, high standards have been set for building sustainably, under tighter budgets and elevated expectations for student housing. The goal is to meet such a broad range of objectives with equal consideration. First, a school must decide on the image it wishes its student housing to portray, before evaluating the factors that will shape the project's direction. This chapter looks at projects particularly successful in balancing interdisciplinary requirements while creating unique architecture.

With so much variety in design options, materials, and building methods, many projects begin with a designated intention to reconsider the direction of student housing design.

Nearly all of the projects featured in this chapter began with a stated intention. These intentions have been tailored to each specific school so that individual housing projects align with an institution's identity, scholastic priorities, or population. They may concern student lifestyle, the school's surroundings, environmental goals, or any other way the school chooses to be portrayed.

There may be many priorities, but a proper balance ensures they are all considered equally and that one priority does not overshadow another. For instance, design decisions should not be based solely on budgetary concerns, but rather should meet budget while also creating the best possible student accommodations. Ultimately, this intention can help focus a project, enabling it to balance multiple priorities successfully, while remaining cohesive. The outcome of these integrated projects is a design that meets all predetermined parameters seamlessly and in such a way that communicates the school's intended message.

Once a goal or an intention has been established, the parameters guiding a project's development are usually evaluated, which may include planners' decisions or circumstantial restrictions. A school may choose to build

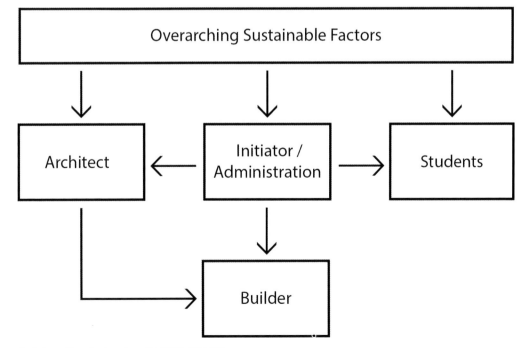

An integrative design development process

sustainably or to increase the area of its public spaces, with budget, construction duration, and size restrictions in mind. Existing surroundings can also mandate guidelines for a project. The existing culture and the urban fabric can influence a project's structure and degree of integration within the local context. When making such evaluations, designers can draw on numerous information sources to help plan around building constraints. They can access studies, polls, and look into students' and faculty feedback. Proper and conscious evaluation of these conditions will lead to a well-integrated initiative.

Once the limitations have been defined, planning methods must consider environmental, economic and societal factors to help meet established requirements. Sustainability can be a subset of a well-balanced project. By definition sustainable development evaluates the built environment as a system of interconnected networks. It takes into consideration the current and long-term needs of a project, and its impact on the environment and society.

Sustainable development principles can be a starting point to achieving balance by helping to analyze various factors. Sustainable design has four pillars, all that must be equally addressed— the environment, the economy, society, and culture. Sustainable design should be flexible, cost-effective, long lasting and multi-functional. It involves connection to the surrounding environment, building with local materials, and ultimately designing for the present and the future (Williams 2007). These four pillars, in addition to being the foundation for sustainable design, can help in the evaluation process for a student housing project in order to help lead to a balanced design.

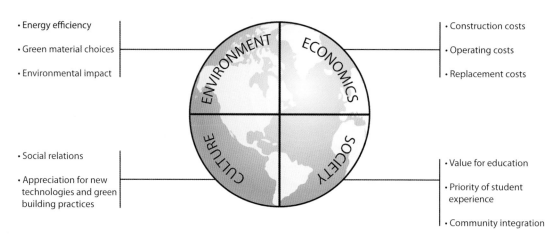

- Energy efficiency
- Green material choices
- Environmental impact

- Construction costs
- Operating costs
- Replacement costs

- Social relations
- Appreciation for new technologies and green building practices

- Value for education
- Priority of student experience
- Community integration

**The four pillars of sustainability and their attributes**

Ideally, the building will be part of a self-sustaining process of activities and resources, without drawing from external sources. For instance, energy needs can be supplied by photovoltaic panels and solar collectors, which heat water. If excess energy is produced, it can be used for communal needs and to power streetlights. Similarly, a self-sustaining water source can be obtained through the collection and purification of rainwater and the integration of a greywater recycling system. This will help reduce the amount of energy used on public water purification.

Sustainability can also be increased by reinforcing the interdependence among the dwellings' subcomponents. If one component can positively affect another, then a supporting relationship will be formed. As more relationships emerge, a network begins to develop. For example, a structure using lower-cost recycled materials not only helps the environment, but also is more affordable to build. Its "green" image may also turn out to be a marketing tool for the school to attract students.

A building should constantly evolve to accommodate the needs of its occupants.

A dwelling that can be refurbished to extend its longevity is more sustainable than one that has a finite life. Therefore, the building's design concept should factor in adaptability to change. If a building is well built, the school's administration saves on maintenance and operational expenses during occupancy. These savings could be invested in new eco-friendly technologies, for instance. A building that is adaptable to its occupants' needs can also be retrofitted, rather than demolished.

As one of the four pillars of sustainability, the environment has become an important factor in contemporary building design and construction (Williams 2007). As technologies advance, they have become increasingly attainable in their integration with new design projects; while diminishing natural resources have also elevated the importance of technologies today. Consideration for the environment within building design includes material selection and the use of alternative energy sources. Some designers work with surrounding nature, local materials and proper waste management. Others use a building's orientation to exploit sun or wind exposure for alternative energy and temperature

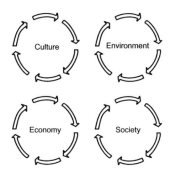 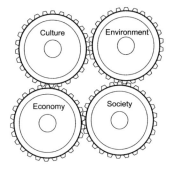 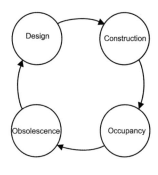

Self-sustaining generators   Supporting relation   Life cycle

Principles of sustainable systems

management. One of the more subtle benefits of "green" design is the impact it has on students as they engage with their built environment, enabling students to advocate environmental preservation in many instances.

Many nations face economic constraints that are unlikely to change in the near future. With increasingly tight school budgets, new student housing must meet this challenge. In part, "green" building may be a smart investment, as it can foster future savings. Construction costs can be managed by using prefabricated components, or modular construction, and by completing projects on time. Good management of future costs may include planning for low maintenance, as well as operating costs. Building within market requirements is also important—by ensuring student housing meets projected enrollment and usage. When appraising the budget, it is vital to properly evaluate the cost benefits of building sustainably in the short and long term (Ekundayo et al 2011). As part of sustainable development, economical choices must be made to meet current demands while simultaneously considering future needs and benefits.

As with any project, student housing must also meet societal demands to be appreciated by its occupants. It must satisfy emerging trends in student housing, paradigm shifts in education, and increasingly diverse student populations. Some projects may even choose to address other societal needs within the residence. For instance, the project could include areas for social housing. The better a project meets societal requirements, the more socially relevant it will remain in the future.

Lastly, culture, another pillar of sustainability, has a profound effect on the success of a design. Buildings that are perceived as poorly designed may be rendered obsolete and will deteriorate rapidly. There must be cultural values in the building practices that support the progression. In a recent survey, it was found that, among high school students intending to attend university in the United States, 68 percent consider a school's commitment to sustainability an important factor when choosing a school (Van Mourik 2012). Therefore, it could be suggested that the current propagation of sustainable buildings may be due to the education and awareness of the public who uphold its importance.

The projects that will be shown in this chapter are successful at balancing many needs, but also stand apart by creating their own architectural language that expresses the interwoven nature of their projects. Whereas early student housing buildings conveyed exclusivity, and those from the mid 20th century were modernist blocks, the projects of today can utilize a wide range of forms and materials to portray the school's intentions. The school's priorities can be shown through differentiation of volumes, inclusions of public spaces on campus, or integration with an existing city. The interior can also express the school's priorities for students through interior layouts and amenities offered. As architectural works, they communicate—through form and aesthetics—the specific message that each school wishes to convey to its population and future students.

Current circumstances have created an environment that requires architectural works to consider many factors. Projects face economic constraints, environmental responsibilities and social and cultural demands. To help guide a housing project, schools can set their own goals or challenges that communicate their message to their desired audience. The exemplary student housing projects that will be shown in this chapter unite multi-disciplinary requirements to seamlessly form unique architectural design.

# Tietgen Dormitory

**Lundgaard & Tranberg Arkitekter** // Nordea-Fonden, Copenhagen, Denmark

The inspiration for this project was a desire to create a space that satisfied the needs of both the individual and the collective. Nordea-Fonden, an organization focused on public and charitable causes, commissioned this student residence. The project has a circular form with projecting volumes. The architects modeled their design after the traditional Tulou round structures of China, which consist of individual dwellings and communal facilities combined in a circular building.

As such, the Tietgen Dormitory is shaped like a seven-story-high rotunda. The first level comprises common facilities, such as a lounge and kitchen, which surround the innermost tree-filled courtyard. The upper levels house the students' units, which all face away from the circular center, offering panoramic views of the nearby channel. The 360 units occupy a space of 288,473 square feet (26,800 square meters).

The apartments are set at different depths, creating an alternating rhythm. The façade is clad with copper, and features glass and varnished American oak partitions. The copper cladding protects the building from weather damage and, with time, will turn light green. The durability of the exterior continues to the interior. The public spaces, like the lounge areas, are made of exposed concrete and poured magnesium flooring. These durable materials facilitate interior maintenance. Eco-friendly birch plywood partitions panels were also used.

Vivid colors were integrated in the design through the use of bright mailboxes, laundry machines and curtains. Therefore, an interesting contrast was created between the natural material and the brightly colored elements. The building also includes bicycle storage, an auditorium and a roof deck. The Tietgen Dormitory integrates communal and individual needs in a durable structure.

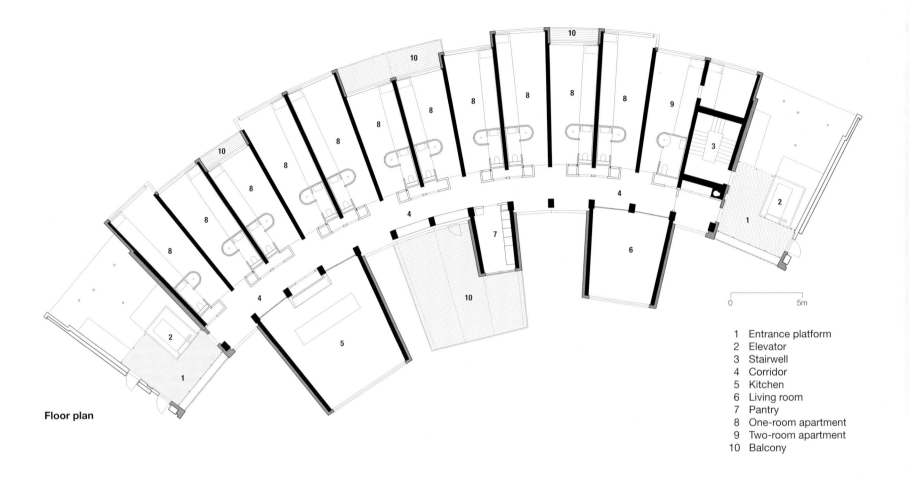

**Floor plan**

1 Entrance platform
2 Elevator
3 Stairwell
4 Corridor
5 Kitchen
6 Living room
7 Pantry
8 One-room apartment
9 Two-room apartment
10 Balcony

0          5m

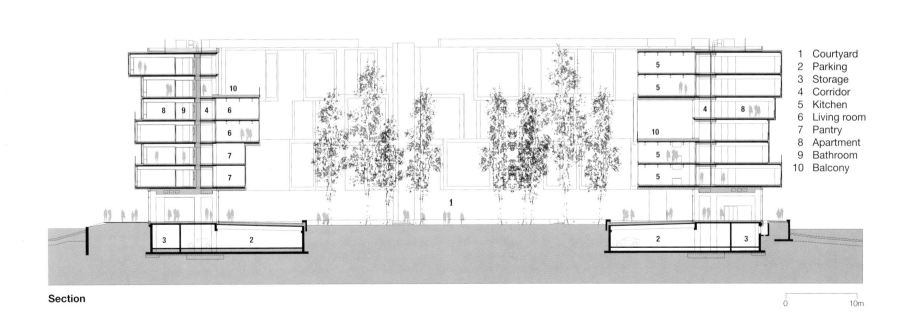

**Section**

1 Courtyard
2 Parking
3 Storage
4 Corridor
5 Kitchen
6 Living room
7 Pantry
8 Apartment
9 Bathroom
10 Balcony

0          10m

# Champion Hill Residences

**GWP Architecture** // Kings College, London, United Kingdom

At Kings College, academic housing and residential accommodations are spread across the center of London and south of the River Thames. The Champion Hill residential campus is located close to Kings College Hospital and Maudsley Hospital in South London—both are university teaching hospitals with associated academic accommodations. A key feature of the site is a Victorian mansion, Platanes, which is a Grade II heritage-listed and protected building. Mature plane trees also define the perimeter of the campus.

To maintain and improve the college's international position, new residential accommodations were required. The basic objective was to create a highly sustainable place for students to live, study, and relax.

Some 746 new study bedrooms are provided by the scheme, which retains the original Victorian mansion as a social hub for the residential campus. The new accommodations provided as en suite study bedrooms in cluster-flat format. Study bedrooms are organized into groups (from five to nine) to give variety to social groupings—each cluster having a shared kitchen/dining/living space. Traditionally, each cluster flat would be self-contained, however this scheme provides student access across each floor. The intent is to encourage social interaction between students and student groups.

The new accommodation has been organized to create four new courtyard spaces within the site, each with its own particular character. One of the courtyards surrounds a mature beech tree. Another incorporates a pond that gathers excess rainwater runoff and provides amenity and increased biodiversity. A central courtyard space provides a focal point, as well as access to each of the new residential blocks and the social hub in Platanes. The large reception rooms to the original Victorian mansion have been restored to provide library, music rooms, games room, media room, bar, and café.

The accommodations were designed to be sustainable, with high levels of insulation, airtight construction and careful specification of construction materials. Benign, natural materials are chosen where possible, including FSC-certified timber, and mechanical ventilation heat recovery (MVHR) mechanisms are provided to all heatable rooms. MVHR systems avoid wasting heat through ventilation while delivering improved internal air quality—removing stale air, excess moisture, and odors.

These highly efficient building specifications result in a minimal energy requirement for space heating. The energy systems that were adopted adhere to the "London Plan" that requires all new buildings to generate a minimum of 20 percent of their energy from renewable sources. Therefore, these new buildings include a self-regulating thermostat and a central combined heat and power (CHP) system—which delivers hot water and electricity— as well as photovoltaic panels on the roofs to generate solar power. Bicycle storage and renting amenities are available to students, which encourages them to adopt more environmentally friendly modes of transportation.

**Block B, ground floor**

The overall scheme achieved a BREEAM 'Outstanding' rating on design-stage assessment, while Platanes received an 'Excellent' rating—a rare result.

The accommodations are reviewed as a learning environment for young people where they are encouraged to live in an environmentally responsible way, and complement the sustainable and energy-efficient features of the buildings.

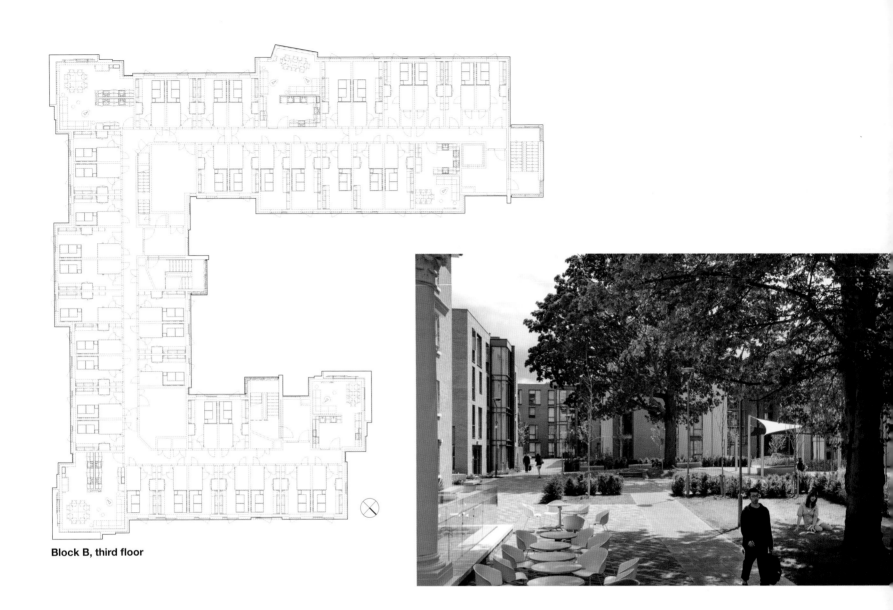

**Block B, third floor**

**Block A, elevation**

# State Street Village

**JAHN** // Illinois Institute of Technology, Chicago, United States

The Illinois Institute of Technology's (IIT) new student residence posed many challenges for the architectural firm Murphy/Jahn, now simply JAHN. First, they had to design for a campus divided in two by the elevated El Train line. Second, the new design had to harmonize with the iconic boxes of steel and glass that Mies Van der Rohe incorporated at IIT in the 1940s and 1950s, spaced within a limited quadrangle area of 110,000 square feet (10,219 square meters). Lastly, the architects were working with a low budget and had to provide adequate housing for 2800 students.

At first, the building appears to have a single unified façade. However, the residence actually comprises three buildings, which are wrapped in corrugated stainless steel. Courtyards and passageways break the linear progression of the buildings. Spaced evenly along a road, the courtyards are shaded spaces, landscaped with perennials and birch trees. Facing the train line, glass screens and thick concrete walls help block the noise. Private rooms, private and semi-private bathrooms, common living and

dining spaces are made available to students. Each wing includes a roof terrace and a common room at the top floor, to encourage communal living.

Long-term energy savings were implemented, such as low-emissivity glass, maximizing daylight, and natural ventilation. Specially

designed furniture systems provide students with comfort and flexibility in arrangement and use. The State Street Village offers its students a harmonized campus space, ecological living quarters, and a courtyard escape within a busy city, in consideration of many aspects of student life.

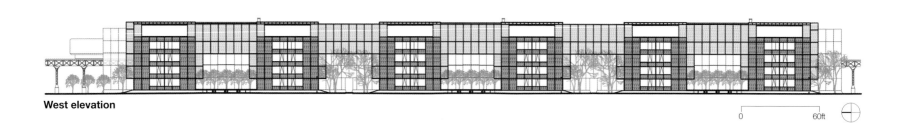

**West elevation**

0            60ft

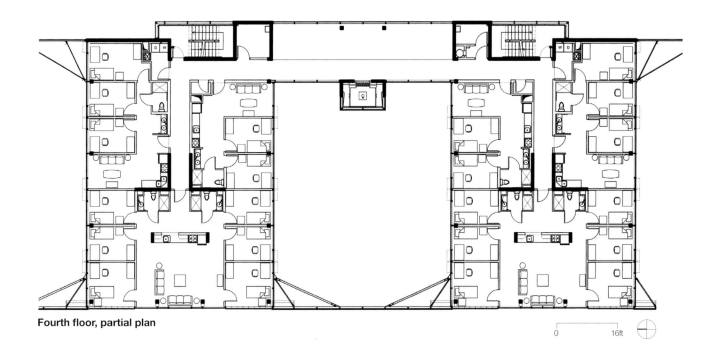

**Fourth floor, partial plan**

0        16ft

# Languedoc

**2A Design (formerly CG Architectes)** // CROUS Rennes Bretagne, Rennes, France

Situated on Languedoc Street in Rennes, this residence comprises 201 student accommodation units, each measuring 218 square feet (20 square meters). The project, by 2A Design (formerly CG Architectes), was part of the urban development of a neighborhood that was designed by L'Atelier de l'île. The building is managed by the public organization CROUS Rennes Bretagne and occupies a space of 63,507 square feet (5900 square meters).

The residence is shaped simply and elegantly, with volumes randomly projecting away from the exterior to create a unique façade. Those projections house spaces such as study rooms, a computer lab, and the cafeteria, all of which are provided with an outdoor view. The spaces jut out of the building as if moving toward the public sphere of the street.

The structure is made of concrete and has two volumes that appear to slide into one another. The volumes have two different façades: one is painted green to relate to its natural surroundings, while the other is dark, which associates the building with the street. The second phase of the project consists of another lower building that is aligned to the street. It contains 38 social housing units.

The building received the Habitat et Environnement—Profil A award, because it responded to seven criteria for this certification, which are based on the environmental quality of the building. A high degree of importance was given to the management of the natural resources that were used, as well as the levels of noise pollution during construction. The project has managed to successfully address diverse concerns, ranging from sustainability to social housing, private and public life.

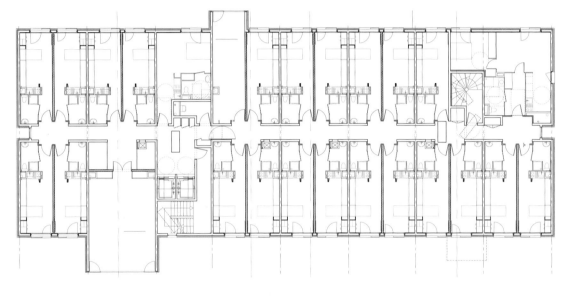

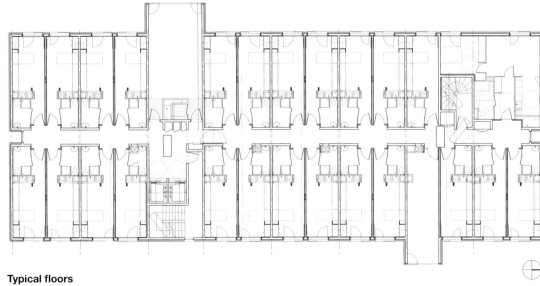

**Typical floors**

# Basket Apartments

**OFIS Arhitekti** // Regie Immobiliere de la Ville de Paris, Paris, France

The building is located on the edge of Parc de la Villette in Paris, wedged between a football field and a tram route. Designed by the Slovenian architecture firm OFIS Arhitekti, this student residence was conceived as part of an urban development plan by Reichen & Robert Architects. The structure is narrow, only 36 feet (11 meters) wide with an area of 10,021 square feet (931 square meters). The building was designed to resemble a stack of wooden baskets. To avoid creating a rectangular building, the designers spanned and rotated the "baskets."

The project is divided into two volumes connected by a narrow bridge that overlooks a small garden. The basement constitutes a mechanical space, while the first floor is used as a common area and the upper nine floors house the students. Every level contains a cluster of rooms with their own balconies.

Each of the buildings' volumes have two different façades, depending on its function. Balconies resembling wooden

baskets punctuate the side facing Rue des Petit Ponts, with their varying orientations creating a dynamic façade. The side facing the football field contains an open passage to the apartment entrance, which is enclosed in a metal mesh. The building is also energy-efficient, as it is well insulated, ventilated and lets in natural light.

The building is composed of 192 studios, each measuring 377 square feet (35 square meters). Each apartment has a similar floor plan including: an entrance, bathroom, wardrobe, kitchenette, workspace, bed and street-facing balcony. Along the length of the adjacent football field, there is an open corridor and a gallery that provides access to the apartments while, at the same time, creating a common space for students. These open spaces also offer a panoramic view of the city and the Eiffel Tower. The Basket Apartments demonstrate that a student residence can integrate sustainability and innovative design, and is not limited to the monotonous forms of some of its predecessors.

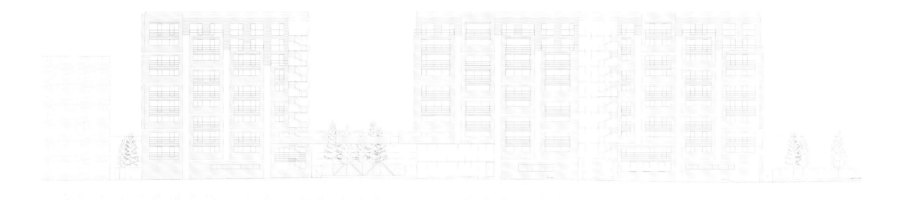

**Elevation**

0         10m

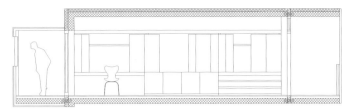

**Section**

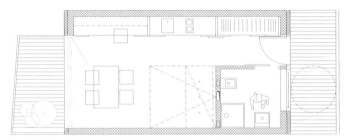

0        2m

**Floor plan**

# UQAM Campus

**Tétreault Parent Languedoc & Saia Barbarese Topouzanov** // Université de Québec à Montréal, Montréal, Canada

The Université de Québec à Montréal (UQAM) is situated at the heart of Montréal's historic alley. In order to benefit from this, the architects created an urban plan that reflected the city's cultural diversity. Completed in 2006, this 53,820-square-foot (5000-square-meter) building includes educational facilities and innovative student housing.

In order to restore the significance of a north-south cultural axis, a new pedestrian walkway was introduced through the site. Thus, the site is divided into two distinct domains—the east and the west. To the west, a series of triangular gardens surrounds the site's existing buildings (including industrial buildings that date back to 1911), which become pavilions in a garden of densely planted trees. The eastern segment includes new structures that are located on the periphery of the campus block.

Many façades throughout the UQAM campus include the university's trademark buff brick. In addition to the aesthetic beauty of this campus, the building dedicated to student

housing is L-shaped and possesses a capacity of 500 students and/or visiting professors. The residence wraps around a private courtyard, which contains planting beds outlined by over-scaled leaves.

This contemporary student housing complex, located within the UQAM campus, is visually engaging, while also including green features and a tremendous capacity of dwellings within its eight-story span.

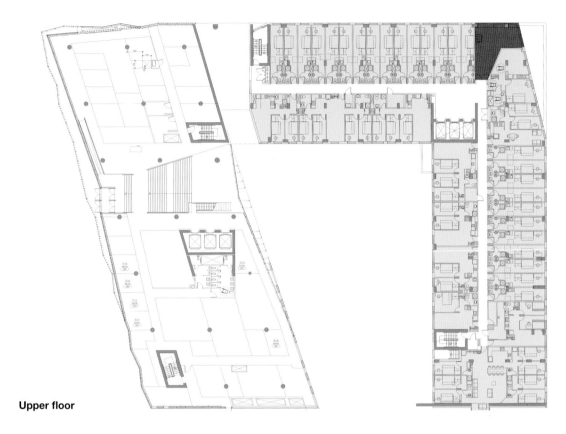

**Upper floor**

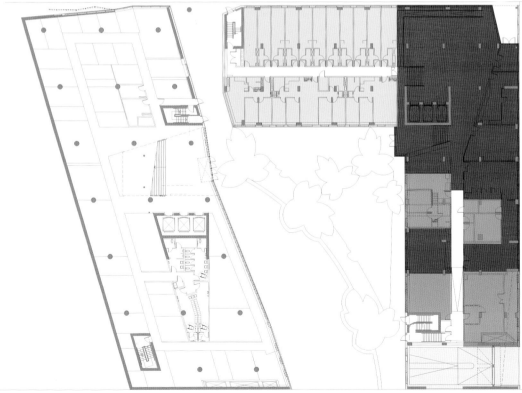

**Ground floor**

# Te Puni Village

**Architectus** // Victoria University, Wellington, New Zealand

The project is located on a steep, sloping site at Victoria University's Wellington campus. The project accommodates 389 students in single-bed dormitory rooms, one-bed studios and two-bedroom apartments.

Te Puni Village is composed of three buildings spread over 145,313 square feet (13,500 square meters). The buildings share a clay tile façade, but in different colors—brown, orange and beige. The Terrace, the Tower and the Edge are linked through a transparent component, which may be regarded as the social organizer of the village. It contains a communal area that includes a dining hall and the village administration.

The first and smallest structure, the Terrace building, faces Fairlie Terrace and is adapted to its surroundings through repetition of the scale and rhythm of the adjacent residential buildings. The Tower building is the tallest and is located in the middle of the site. The third building faces, and forms the edge of, a playing field, hence the name—the Edge.

The entries to the building are located on lower levels of the sloping site. In fact, the site is integral to shaping the layout of the village. During the design process, consideration was given to earthquake damage avoidance, sustainability and maximization of space. For instance, when the students are not in residences, the communal spaces such as the dining hall and the social areas can be rented out, providing another source of income for the university. Te Puni Village is designed to be durable and economic, demonstrating that the two characteristics need not contradict one another.

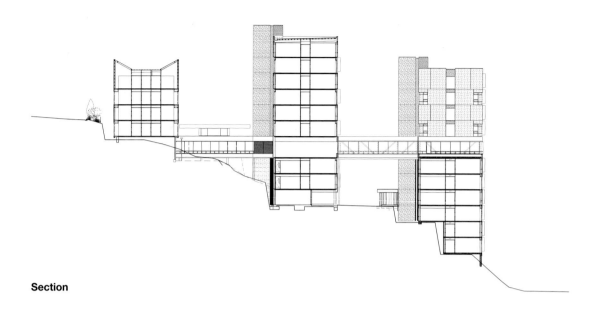

**Section**

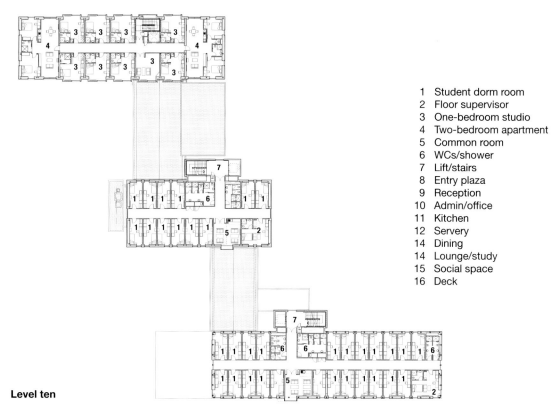

1 Student dorm room
2 Floor supervisor
3 One-bedroom studio
4 Two-bedroom apartment
5 Common room
6 WCs/shower
7 Lift/stairs
8 Entry plaza
9 Reception
10 Admin/office
11 Kitchen
12 Servery
14 Dining
14 Lounge/study
15 Social space
16 Deck

**Level ten**

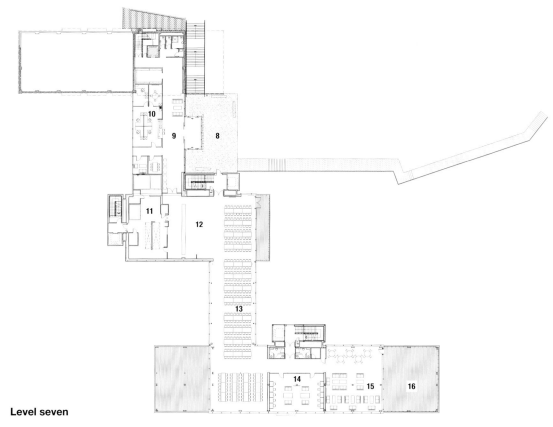

**Level seven**

# Student Housing Poljane

**Bevk Perović Arhitekti** // Ljubljana University, Ljubljana, Slovenia

This student housing project by Bevk Perović Arhitekti is located in the city of Ljubljana, near the Ljubljanica riverbank. The structure comprises both student residences and public facilities for the university's use. The residences provide 56 student accommodations. The student residences and the public spaces occupy a total floor area of 139,931 square feet (13,000 square meters).

The student units are housed in two vertical slabs that sit on top of a horizontal transparent base. The vertical slabs are clad with aluminum, and the dwellings are screened from the street by folding panels of perforated aluminum. The folding screens break the monotony of the façade, contribute to the reduction of noise from the street, and provide privacy to the student bedrooms. The units have wide windows overlooking the street, which also help vary the façade.

The student units surround central services such as bathrooms, kitchens and dining rooms. The kitchen and dining areas overlook the street. The perforations in the panels allow

natural light to pass in, providing students with a well lit but concealed space. The horizontal transparent base includes space for teaching, studying, communal living and leisure. There is also a bicycle parking area on the first floor. By combining university public spaces and residences, students have quick access to all the services they need.

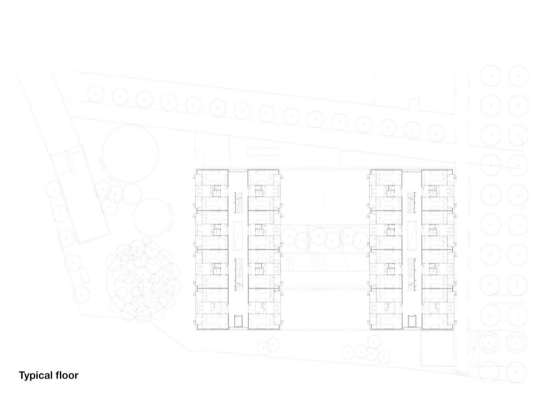

**Typical floor**

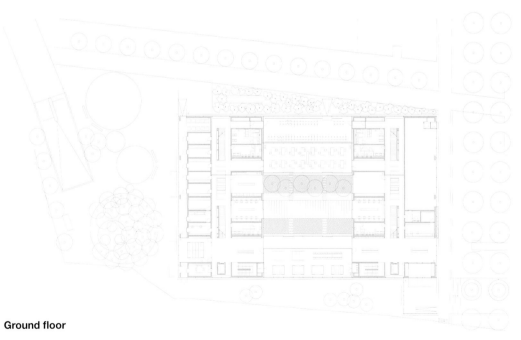

**Ground floor**

# Colegio Mayor Sant Jordi

**Mateo Arquitectura** // University of Barcelona, Barcelona, Spain

The Colegio Mayor Sant Jordi of the University of Barcelona is a student residence offering up to 240 accommodations in 135 rooms. The residence is composed of a tall residential block and a lower block, which serves as the public area. The blocks occupy an area of 131,912 square feet (12,255 square meters).

The project, divided into three volumes, is bordered by open green space to the north and a street to the west. The first volume, the base, is intended for community use. The second and tallest volume comprises the student units. Lastly, the third volume includes sports facilities, a director's office and spare rooms.

The students' residences are covered in metallic façades with folding panels that serve as windows. The architects decided to use

glass and metal as the major materials for the project, which differentiate the Colegio Mayor Sant Jordi from its neighboring residential buildings. The façade is punctuated with color in contrast to the mainly gray façade. This use of color adds a lively character to the university, and is the work of the artist Sílvia Hornig.

Inside the residences, the bedrooms are mostly doubles with a private bathroom. The units also have room for desk space. The common areas, located in the lower block, appear light, transparent and colorful, and house student services such as a meeting hall, dining room, library, bar, game room and a study area. The Colegio Mayor Sant Jordi combines both a residential and public program, responding fittingly to the modern needs of the university and the students.

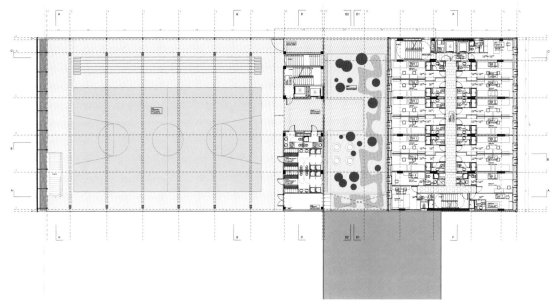

**First floor**

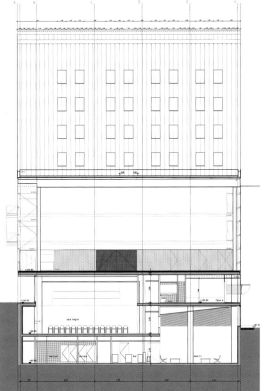

**Section**

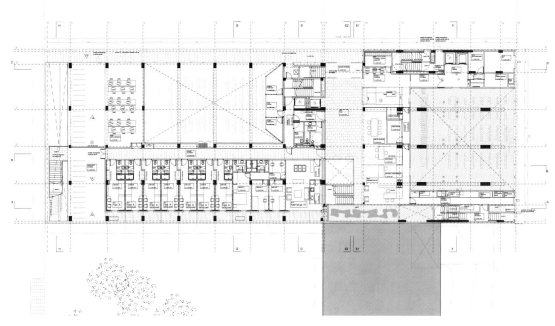

**Ground floor**

# Résidence Étudiante et Résidence Médicalisée

**Emmanuel Combarel Dominic Marrec Architectes** // Espacil Habitat—L'Amicale du Nid, Epinay-sur-Seine, France

Espacil Habitat, a real estate enterprise, and L'Amicale du Nid, an organization committed to helping vulnerable young people, commissioned this residence. The project responds to three different needs and comprises a residence for 170 students in 150 units, 19 accommodations for researchers or invited professors, and social housing for women in distress. The complex occupies a surface of 95,800 square feet (8900 square meters), in four distinct wings.

Each wing is a different color, with green, blue, red, and orange courtyards separating them, while the exterior of the complex is brown and green. The wings are oriented east–west to reduce noise pollution from the adjacent roads, and each courtyard integrates garden areas. The structure engages with the existing neighborhood from the exterior, while offering residents a quiet sanctuary in the courtyards, which is protected from the pressures of an urban landscape.

The structure was split into four volumes, in order to foster the coordination of separate management systems and distinct identities for each wing. The courtyards between the wings create areas for occupants to socialize. The complex includes private study rooms, laundry facilities, indoor and outdoor space for relaxation, and gardens with fruit trees. The project successfully responds to the needs of three types of residents, undertaking the challenge of providing both privacy and identity in each type of residence.

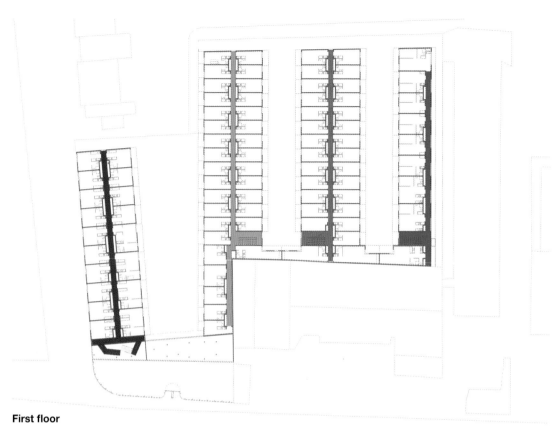

**First floor**

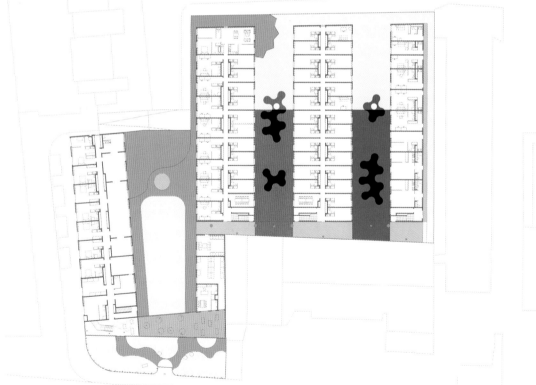

**Ground floor**

RÉSIDENCE ÉTUDIANTE ET RÉSIDENCE MÉDICALISÉE

# Ernie Davis Hall

**Mack Scogin Merrill Elam Architects** // Syracuse University, Syracuse, New York, United States

Ernie Davis Hall is the first sustainable residence built on the Syracuse University campus. Named after one of the university's most memorable athletes, it is also the first student housing project to be constructed on the campus since 1966. Completed in August 2009, the site combines student comfort, amenities (to encourage a healthy-living style) and eco-friendly features, involving efficient energy use and conservation.

Located on the corner of the sloped Comstock Avenue and University Place, the residential complex enjoys close proximity to the quadrangle and the lawn, as well as sharing a south courtyard with the adjacent Dell Plain Residence Hall.

The nine-story building provides students with a large academic space, including a three-terraced-level dining space, a large fitness center and a convenience store. Those recreational units are connected to each other by one inclined interior sidewalk, where visitors and students can socialize and find relief from exterior elements.

Twenty four student rooms, as well as lounges and laundry rooms, are found on every residential level. Each floor was designed with operable windows, placed strategically in order to receive a maximum of daylight, while offering enhanced views on the surrounding city.

The building was planned to minimize energy consumption–with features such as a concrete structure, the white roof of the residence, an innovative heating and cooling system, and an energy-efficient dishwashing system. Low-flow plumbing fixtures and stormwater retention systems also allow for an efficient use of water.

Efforts to design a sustainable student housing community have won the Ernie Davis Hall a Leadership in Energy and Environmental Design (LEED) Gold rating. It marked the Syracuse University's first step toward a "greener", more ecologically concerned campus. In addition, the residence design created new socialization opportunities for the students and redefined the comfort of a student's life, illustrating that achieving both a comfortable residence and environmental health is an attainable goal in student housing.

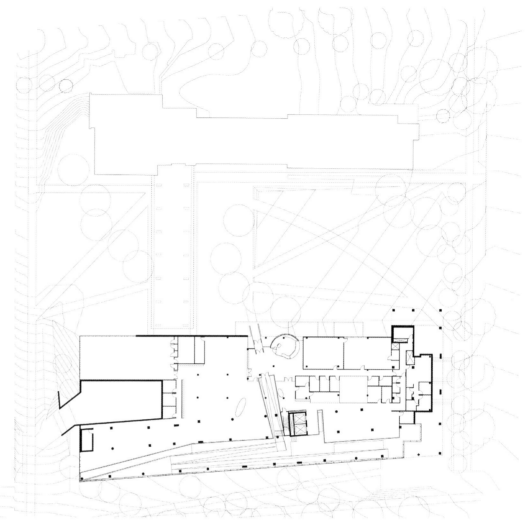

**Level 2**

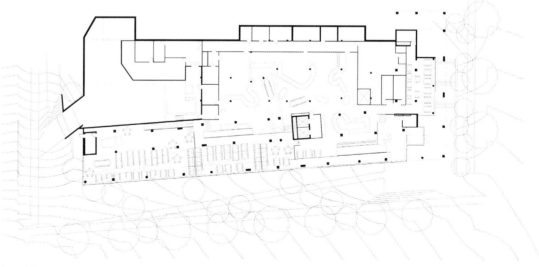

**Level 1**

# 04 Green Residences

A decision to build an environmentally sustainable building will be made early on in the design process. The designers may choose to include several "green" systems or pursue a single strategy thoroughly (for example, power with solar energy). Choices may vary according to priorities, budget, or requirements dictated by the local context and pre-existing regulations. This chapter presents the advantages of having green buildings, describes green ratings, and outlines new technologies that can be used in contemporary student housing.

As public environmental awareness grows, standards need to be maintained to ensure the quality of green construction methods and techniques, and to avoid false claims, which often arise in unregulated consumer products or services. Leadership in Energy and Environmental Design (LEED) is one of the most widely used and recognized programs that certify green buildings. The program comprises levels of certification (assigned according to a points system), which are awarded to a variety of categories that may be certified silver, gold or platinum.

As of 2014, certified projects can be found in 140 countries and territories on all continents (Holmes 2014).

Another similar certification program is the Building Research Establishment Environmental Assessment Methodology (BREEAM). It serves as an environmental assessment method and a rating system for buildings. It is used in fifty countries and has over one million buildings registered and 250,000 certified (BREEAM n.d.). Prior to adding efficiency and green technologies to a building, BREEAM also encourages intelligent design, inspired by low carbon and minimal energy demands. Since LEED and BREEAM are widely recognized, certification can potentially attract prospective students, increase a school's reputation, or increase the competition between schools. These certifications, in their very existence, also ensure the future of green building. Depending on the source of funding—through the government or initiated by the schools themselves—institutions may require that new buildings will obtain a certain level of green certification.

Some add-on technologies can make a building more environmentally friendly, such as low-flow toilets, material choices, light fixtures, and energy-efficient appliances. However, for new constructions to be environmentally friendly, architects and planners need to consider the local environmental context. Strategies such as

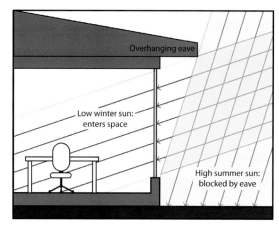

Using passive design principles for summer and winter sun

the orientation and shape of the building can be used to maximize passive solar gain, natural light or ventilation.

Although having sunlight is often essential in warming the buildings during winter, exposure to sun should be limited in summer to avoid overheating and reduce dependency on central cooling systems. This can be achieved in two ways. The first concerns the width of the roof's overhang. Since the altitude of the sun varies between summer and winter, the overhang can be adjusted so that it shades the dwelling from summer rays while allowing winter sunlight to enter. The second way is to plant trees, or utilize existing ones, along the sunlit side of the building. Different species of trees also have various levels of transparency. Trees that allow more light to pass through when they are bare during winter are preferable. When faced with a choice between bare coniferous and bare deciduous trees, for example, the deciduous

trees would make a more sustainable choice, offering 50 percent transparency, while coniferous trees only allow 8 percent transparency. Choosing deciduous trees also allows more sun into the dwelling during winter months while shading the dwelling from the sun during the summer. The chosen tree species should also be native to the area and the climatic conditions. For example, choosing to plant coniferous trees in arid places would not be sustainable due to the scarcity of water.

Green strategies and technologies have greatly improved in recent decades. For instance, green roofs are now fairly common and can be used in various climates and environments. They are a smart choice for schools looking to reduce future energy and repair costs while visibly advocating their green initiatives. Green roofs can grow many plants, and can be intensive or extensive for smaller or larger plant life.

Such strategies and technologies come with a long list of benefits. They reduce the "heat island effect" in metropolitan areas caused by vast zones of heat-absorbing asphalt and concrete, and help manage stormwater through absorption, reducing the inundation on sewer systems (University of Idaho n.d.). Roof lifespans are extended with green roofs, due to a reduction in drastic temperature fluctuations, which can damage roofing materials (Gittleman n.d.). The surrounding air quality also improves because the plants filter air pollution and provide oxygen. Finally, green roofs act as insulation for a building, reducing internal heating and cooling energy demands (Gittleman n.d.).

There are campuses that provide other types of gardening initiatives. Spaces can be provided in areas on campus for students to garden their own small crops. This promotes nutrition

Intensive

Extensive

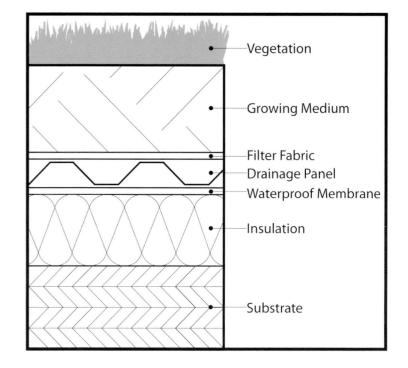

"Green" roof systems (left) and a roof's cross section (right)

A greywater recycling system

and education about sustainable environments. While the green roof costs are more expensive than traditional roofs, they are investments with benefits that initiate future savings.

In some parts of the world, water is an increasingly scarce resource, and limiting its use is another green strategy, if not a vital necessity. Areas that are subject to water scarcity, such as southern California in the United States, can take advantage of technologies that allow for rainwater harvesting and greywater recycling. Greywater is used water from sinks, showers and washing machines. It can be filtered onsite and reused to flush toilets or irrigate surrounding plants. Multi-unit housing, such as student housing, is optimal for greywater recycling since the generation of greywater usually exceeds the required amount for toilet use (Zadeh et al 2012). There are also water-saving measures that can be used in any location to minimize water waste, such as low-flow fixtures and toilets. Although the benefits of water savings are clear, most greywater systems are only found in schools that are located in areas dealing with water shortages.

The choice of building materials will also affect the environmental impact of a project and can determine energy consumption during occupancy. Materials that require low energy levels for their production, known as embedded energy, should be selected. Designers can choose to use locally sourced or fabricated materials, which minimizes the resources required for transportation. Alternatively, they may choose to use a construction method that reduces waste, such as prefabricated components or modular construction. Materials from demolished buildings can be reused in new constructions or brought for recycling in order to diminish waste.

Many building materials—such as concrete, bricks, glass and metals—can be made with recycled components. Under some circumstances, this may reduce emissions and energy needs by as much as 90 percent (Metcalf 2011). If natural materials such as wood are desired, they can be purchased from well-managed forests to ensure that trees are harvested sustainably. Another contributing factor in material choice is lifespan; choosing materials that are durable will reduce replacement or maintenance costs.

Today's student housing is designed to meet the occupants' needs. As most of their time will be spent indoors, there is new awareness of indoor air quality (IAQ), which may affect the long term health of the users. Interior material choices can also have environmental impacts. There are thousands of indoor materials that can emit toxins in the form of gases, known as volatile organic compounds (VOCs), which may affect inhabitants and the environment (The U.S. Environmental Protection Agency 2012). The most common products are paints, adhesives, cleaning supplies, many building materials and furnishings (The U.S. Environmental Protection

Agency 2012). There are new options for materials that are low-VOC or VOC-free, which are available as alternatives. These materials will also have less pollutant effects when they are eventually discarded.

Some products such as carpets, particleboard, and other manufactured wood products, are subject to standard testing procedures, the results of which can be compared. Manufacturers of these products who do not disclose full emission test reports should be considered with skepticism, if being considered at all. In cases where testing is not common or standardized, the manufacturer should disclose the product's contents and a description of the manufacturing processes and treatments that are likely to affect its emissions. The willingness of manufacturers to take steps to improve a product's performance in terms of reducing harmful emissions should also be taken into consideration in the selection process. For instance, pretreatment and the aeration of a product, prior to its installation in a building, could significantly improve that product's IAQ performance.

It should also be mentioned that considerations for good IAQ are not limited to construction. Many furnishings are made of particleboard products or have lacquered finishes that have high emission levels, sometimes for long periods after construction. While furniture selection is usually beyond the responsibility of either the architect or the builder, it might be useful to include suggestions in an owner's manual, along with recommendations for cleaning products and the maintenance of ventilating equipment.

With finite supplies of fossil fuels, energy costs are rising and many innovative schools are designing their new student housing projects to rely on renewable energy sources, namely solar and wind, to save on energy costs. These energy systems can be installed in any school, in most climates. Alternative energies are already flourishing in Europe and they are growing in popularity in the North American market (Cost of Solar n.d.). Globally, the solar industry installed 50 gigawatts of capacity in 2011, exceeding 100 gigawatts by 2012 (Lacey 2013), while projections show exponential growth is expected to continue. Moreover, in 2014 the price of solar panels in the United States had decreased by half since 2008, while installation was often paired with government incentives to further reduce costs (Cost of Solar n.d.). With these technologies more readily available at lower costs, it is becoming more reasonable to see them installed in schools.

The future is pointing to self-sustaining, ecological, longer-lasting buildings. It is expected that universities will remain up-to-date with new green technologies, as they have the ability to expose new generations to their benefits. Student housing can be used as a learning laboratory that can continually educate students about sustainable living, and how to live within their local environments with minimal impact. Schools need to build with the long term future in mind, in order to save costs. In addition, such measures will also appeal to prospective students, and portray a contemporary and relevant mindset. It is a constant struggle to integrate new technologies, local environmental requirements and aesthetically pleasing designs. The following student housing examples will demonstrate how environmentally friendly construction can enhance a school's appeal.

# Sustainable Student Residences

**GWP Architecture** // County and Grizedale Colleges, Lancaster University, Lancaster, United Kingdom

Lancaster University is located on a 360-acre (146-hectare) campus to the south of the historic city of Lancaster. The campus maintains the original master plan, with a perimeter access road, serving academic and residential accommodations, and a central pedestrian route through the campus, linking university buildings. The university is organized on a collegiate basis and the student residential accommodations were designed for County and Grizedale Colleges.

The Lancaster Sustainable Student Residences were designed in response to a university brief for the accommodations, which required three key outcomes in addition to spatial and specification standards. They were: improved product performance (sustainability and the environment), enhanced living space and social provision/experience, and lower rent proposition (lower delivery and running costs).

The unit accommodations are provided as a mix of conventional four-story cluster-flat format and a new accommodation solution based on the four-story "townhouse" format.

The cluster-flat accommodations comprise six en suite units, sharing common kitchen, dining and living spaces. Townhouse accommodation allocates the whole of the first floor as social living space for 12 students, with direct access to external amenity space. The three floors above provide four units per floor with amenities shared between every two units. This scheme represented the first example of townhouse-based student accommodations, and has become increasingly popular with universities and students.

The organization of outdoor space is carefully considered, with the inclusion of courtyards in keeping with the historic university residences of the United Kingdom. The accommodations for Grizedale College are organized within a collection of semi-private courtyards and a "public" square, which leads to the central pedestrian route through the campus. The residential accommodations at County College are organized in a similar manner, also creating a large open space at the northern end of the pedestrian route.

The energy strategy is based on a "fabric first" approach, delivering a highly insulated and airtight building envelope. This strategy includes the use of mechanical ventilation and heat recovery (MVHR) systems that provide fresh, filtered air, and manage humidity levels, as well as the reduction of space required for solar thermal collectors that provide hot water. The MVHR systems operate in excess of 80 percent recovery efficiency.

Careful attention was also given to the construction process, which was based on panelized timber frame assembly, and extensive offsite manufacture of the building shell and amenities pods. This efficient construction strategy generated cost benefits and significantly reduced waste during construction. FSC-certified timber was also used throughout. A variety of measures were adopted to ensure healthy environmental conditions, particularly indoor air quality, levels of natural light and improved acoustic performance. Wherever possible, natural and benign materials are used internally, that can be easily recycled and do not emit unwanted VOCs.

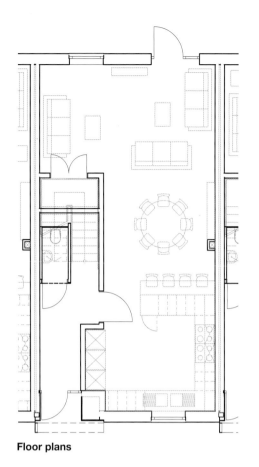
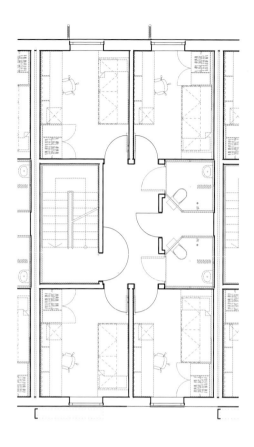

**Floor plans**

The residential accommodations achieved a
BREEAM 'Excellent' rating and the BREEAM UK
national award in the multi-residential category.
The project received eight other awards.
Lancaster Sustainable Student Residences
offer these award-winning accommodations
as part of the educational offering.

# The Residential Life Project

**Carrier Johnson + Culture** // Pitzer College, Claremont, United States

The Residential Life Project was a complete reimagining of student residences at Pitzer College. The project, built in two phases, called for innovative and ecological new student residences. Three halls were built in phase one, housing 318 students in double rooms. Phase two accommodates 300 additional students in four residences.

The residences are low-rise buildings, only three and four stories, and clad in the warm, neutral tones of stucco. The façades are intersected with shaded porches, made from wood, with orange doors. The college sits at the foothills of the Angeles National Forest, offering spectacular views on Mount Baldy and Mount San Antonio.

More than 40 sustainable systems and technologies have been integrated throughout the buildings. Solar panels were mounted, along with green roofs and living walls, which help insulate the buildings thermally while reducing the amount of rainwater runoff. This lowers the "heat island" effect. In the phase two residences, there is a greywater system,

which treats water from showers and sinks for use in outdoor landscape irrigation. There are also stormwater retention basins that have been installed to capture rainwater runoff.

The residences were constructed from recycled materials, including the structural steel, concrete, gypsum board, carpeting, and insulation. The construction waste was reused or recycled. The heating and cooling system incorporates high-efficiency chillers, boilers and pumps to lower energy consumption, and natural ventilation is available throughout the residences.

The first phase of the project was awarded the US Green Building Council's Leadership in Energy and Environmental Design (LEED) Gold certification. The second phase earned LEED Platinum certification. Students have access to computer labs, classrooms, and study rooms. The Residential Life Project illustrates that ecological design is an accessible goal for designers of student residences, and that a small carbon footprint does not mean sacrificing students' quality of life.

THE RESIDENTIAL LIFE PROJECT

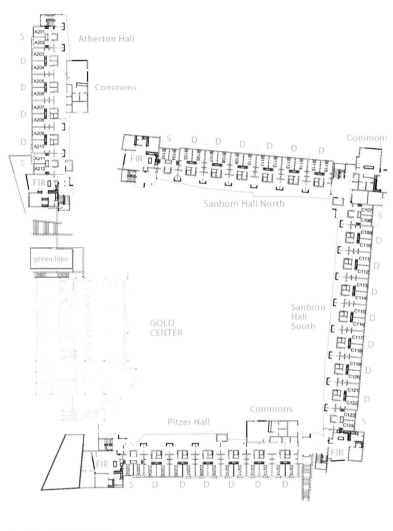

D = Double Room Suite
S = Single Room Suite

**Phase 1, Level 2**

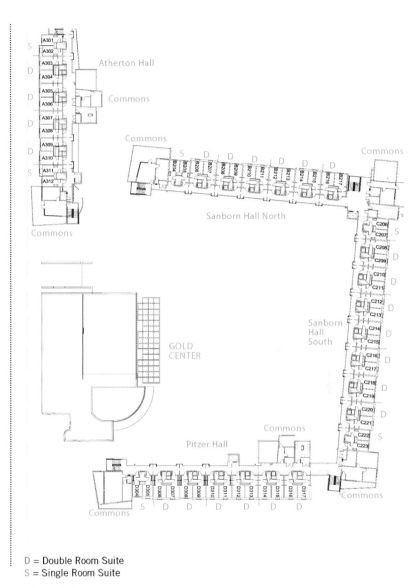

D = Double Room Suite
S = Single Room Suite

**Phase 1, Level 3**

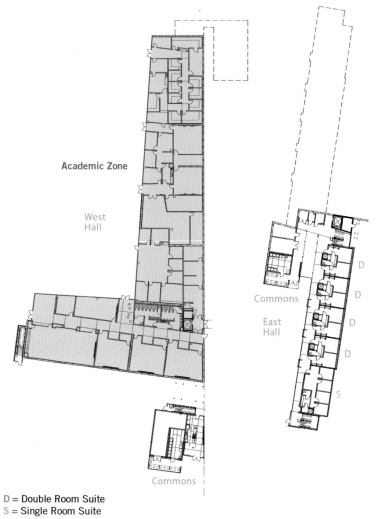

**Academic Zone**

West
Hall

Commons

East
Hall

D
D
D
D
D
S

D = Double Room Suite
S = Single Room Suite

**Phase 2, Level 1**

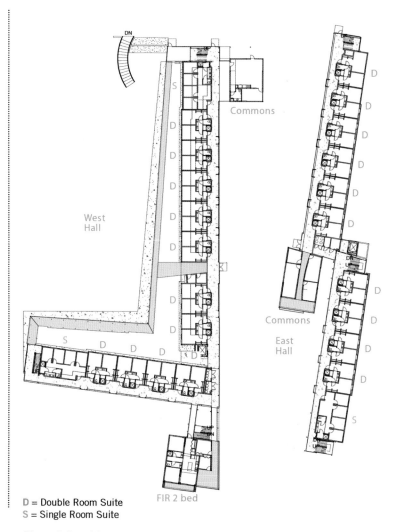

DN

Commons

West
Hall

D
D
D
D
D
D
D
D
S
D D D D D

FIR 2 bed

Commons

East
Hall

D
D
D
D
D
D
D
D
S

D = Double Room Suite
S = Single Room Suite

**Phase 2, Level 2**

# Ungdomsboliger Aarhus Havn

**ARKITEMA Architects** // Ringgaarden Housing Association, Aarhus, Denmark

This student accommodation, designed by ARKITEMA Architects, is a highly energy-efficient building. The design is the outcome of an architectural competition, which was won by the firm in 2011. Ringgaarden Housing Association, a non-profit organization, commissioned the residence to be built in the city of Aarhus's harbor area. The harbor was chosen as it is an area in development, and the association wanted to encourage the growth of a diverse population in a new urban quarter. The 99 student units are contained in a 12-story-tall structure with a total floor area of 52,743 square feet (4900 square meters).

The façade facing the boulevard consists of solar cells that are integrated as balcony guardrails. Two guardrails are linked together to create a frame that emulates the framing of the windows on the other three façades. These solar panels also serve as a shield against noise and sun.

The majority of the apartments are composed of two rooms, with windows of different sizes, which provide an even distribution of light in the units, and frame the view.

The project uses thick insulation and high-strength white concrete to reduce heat loss and lower energy consumption. This student residence is an excellent example of unique ecological initiatives that can be integrated in the design of student housing.

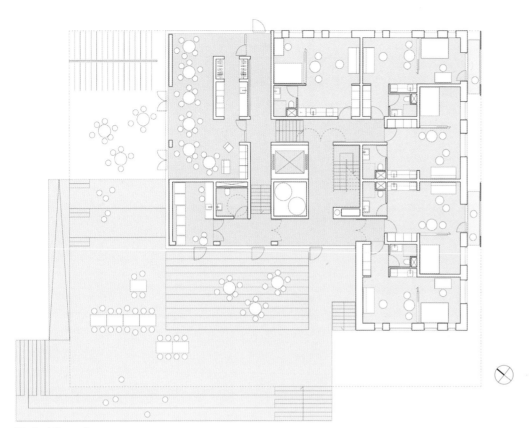

**Typical floor plan**

# Student Guest House

**be baumschlager eberle** // University of Vienna, Vienna, Austria

When completed in 2005, this student housing was the first to be built to the passive house standard in Austria and was one of the largest passive houses in Europe, occupying an area of 68,125 square feet (6329 square meters).

The building was designed to accommodate over 800 international students and is located in Vienna's historic center. The design fits well in its environment, which consists mainly of 19th-century classical buildings. The massive façade has high-quality windows and copper window shutters that reflect vernacular Viennese architecture. When all the shutters are closed, the Student Guest House becomes more of a sculpture than a building.

The residence's technical system consists of mechanical ventilation based on a geothermal energy source and heat recovery. Rockwool insulation is used to optimize the indoor climate and protect against sound pollution. Solar energy and passive preheating of fresh air also contribute to the reduction of energy consumption in the Student Guest House. Natural light enters the building through the windows to create an illuminated interior space and save on artificial lighting costs. Students living here benefit from the sustainable initiatives of the Student Guest House construction.

# Charles David Keeling Apartments

**KieranTimberlake** // University of California (San Diego), La Jolla, United States

This project is named after a leading scientist in the field of carbon dioxide emissions and the greenhouse effect. As a result, the designers set as a goal to address Southern California's environmental challenges. The Charles David Keeling Apartments are located on the southwestern edge of the University of California's San Diego campus, overlooking the cliffs of La Jolla. Second-year students were previously located further from the main dining hall. This project regrouped their dwellings nearer to several communal facilities.

The Keeling Apartments are composed of three buildings in a C-shape that are placed around a central courtyard, housing a total of 510 students and occupying an area of 147,000 square feet (13,657 square meters).

The apartment buildings resemble the rest of UC San Diego's campus, with exterior walkways, a warm color palette and repeating sunscreens. The cast-in-place concrete structure may resemble existing campus buildings, but they are innovative in their use of practices and systems that reduce the consumption of energy.

The apartment units are well lit and ventilated, with 90 percent of all regularly occupied spaces receiving high daylight coverage. The exterior contains shading devices that regulate solar heat gain. The "green" roof is covered with vegetation, which absorbs rainwater, provides insulation, and diminishes the "heat island" effect. A photovoltaic system is also located on the roof, and it provides 6 percent of the building's energy. Rainwater and greywater are also recycled on the student campus. Finally, landscaping on the ground level includes retention ponds and bioswales that retain rainwater.

The buildings have been awarded the Leadership in Energy and Environmental Design for New Construction (LEED-NC) Platinum certification. It is the first LEED Platinum student housing in the University of California system. These pioneering apartments beautifully improve the UC San Diego campus.

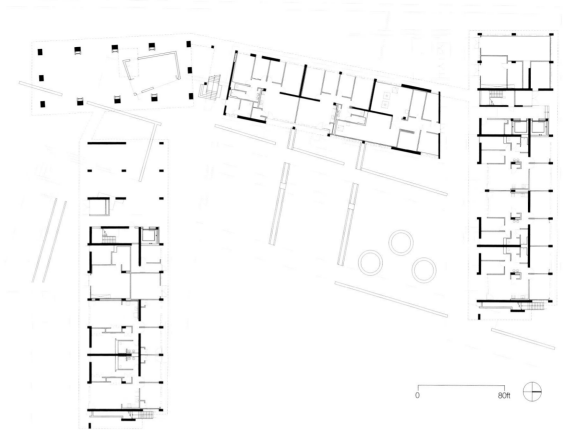

**First floor plan**

# Boston University Sydney Academic Centre

**Tony Owen Partners and Silvester Fuller** // Boston University, Chippendale, Australia

The residence is located in Sydney and comprises 175 bedrooms. Silvester Fuller proposed the design concept, while Tony Owen Partners saw the project to completion. The university commissioned the residence in order to improve the dwelling standards of visiting students. The eight-story-tall energy-efficient building contains three lecture halls, a library, lounge, rooftop terrace, and an adjoining communal kitchen and café.

The project appears to float above a transparent first level, while the rest of the façade is clad in brick. The principle feature of the project is the canyon-like slots in the façade, which let sunlight and ventilation penetrate the building's interior. The windows in the slots are made in the shape of a rhomboid to maximize their efficiency. The end walls of the slots are seven stories tall and are made of glass louvers. These louvers, operable on every level, allow fresh air to enter the building, reducing the internal ambient temperature, thereby diminishing the need for air conditioning.

According to architect Tony Owen, the air passes through the buildings as if it had gills, thereby permitting them to ventilate naturally As a result, the energy-efficient design creates a highly sustainable student residence.

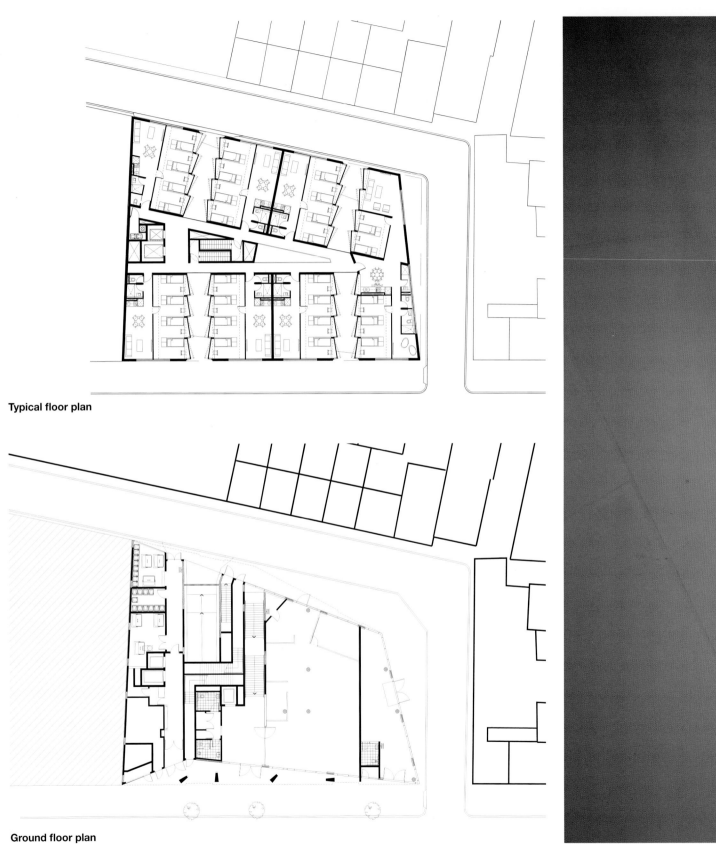

**Typical floor plan**

**Ground floor plan**

# 05 Student Life

As it is often their first experience away from home, many students may expect the same living conditions they have grown accustomed to with their parents, while requiring the space to learn and create their own new communities. Some schools even regard student residences as an opportunity to influence the wellbeing, personal and psychosocial development of their students. This chapter looks at the living experience in students' accommodations and the solutions that designers utilize to better serve those needs.

As needs of contemporary students are ever-changing, the traditional residence hall is no longer a satisfactory model of accommodation. Today's students look for access to technology, quiet study spaces, and opportunities for social engagement after hours. A way to meet these requirements is for architecture firms and schools to treat the student population as the client and partner in the design process (Anchors and Winston 1993). They can ascertain the ways that students prefer to live and seek student input prior to, or during, design. After reviewing certain projects, it seems that most schools share a common goal of limiting social isolation and facilitating relationships, while creating a home-like

The common study area in the Tietgen Dormitory, Copenhagen, Denmark

environment. They often attempt to create an environment that integrates domesticity with study space.

The concept of *community* is fairly new in student housing. In a student residence, a community is seen as a way to encourage a sense of belonging and the formation of relationships among newcomers. Socializing is emphasized in many housing projects, but to properly encourage socialization, students need to be able to retreat into their private lives as and when they wish. A proper design can help achieve a balance between community and individuality. The planning and division of spaces is an integral tool in defining these public and private areas. For example, allocating large spaces for gatherings (both indoors and outdoors), including study spaces and shared meal facilities, and making spaces for extracurricular activities and entertainment in the building. These common spaces encourage students to gather, socialize and exchange ideas as part of their learning process. Private spaces are also important, ensuring quiet areas for studying, reading, or for more intimate gatherings. These spaces can be provided for within students' rooms, but also by subdividing larger public spaces. Providing various spaces to accommodate different needs, at all times of the day, will be more successful in attracting and maintaining occupancy. There is a symbiotic relationship between a student's private and social life, which if well balanced, can help achieve a comfortable, home-like atmosphere.

Schools now have several choices in systematically planning for their student communities. For example, they can plan for student populations with diverse personal needs, including those with reduced mobility, so that their communities are both inclusive and pluralistic. Housing can be subdivided according to floors, wings, or an entire building. Small neighborhoods or villages can be created through architecture and administrative planning, with shared services and activities (Peterkin 2013). Students can be surveyed and placed according to their preferred living conditions, their year or age group, by program of study, or according to special interests (Peterkin 2013). These divisions are not meant to be restrictive or to create subgroups, but rather a method many schools use to create a less intimidating

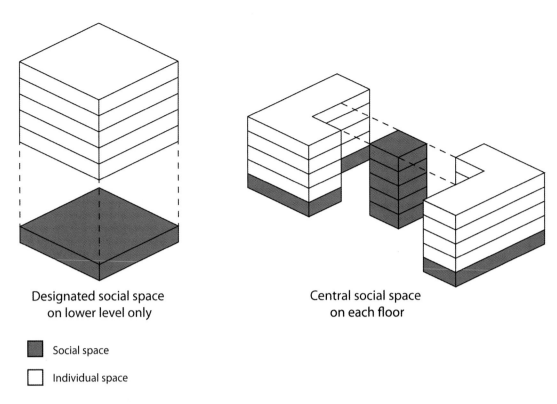

**Designated social space on lower level only**

**Central social space on each floor**

■ Social space

□ Individual space

**Individual and shared social spaces in student housing**

social environment. If the project is of a smaller scale, this may not be necessary. When some schools have accumulated housing units that are smaller in scale, the units themselves become communities (McGill University n.d.). These communities of students can have shared common and study spaces. They can have organized activities on and off school grounds. The outcome will be a sense of belonging and enthusiasm, leading to an environment conducive to learning through social interactions and exchange between a diverse range of people.

Student housing provides opportunities for new social interactions but it can also be used to teach young people practical life skills as they live on their own for the first time. In the past, schools appropriated the missing parental role through authoritarian management of their

students (Anchors and Winston 1993; Anchors, Branch Douglas and Kasper 1993). This approach has now changed and it is thought that greater independence allows young people to mature. On an individual level, independence teaches students about time management, proper study techniques, how to be responsible and how to succeed on their own. On a larger scale, residences may include some self-run facilities that leave students in charge of their own management. For instance, shared kitchen areas require cleaning, while student-run shops or supply stores teach responsibility and organization. Students can also form groups to manage activities, their lounge areas, outdoor spaces and online groups. The architecture of the student housing can offer spaces for such activities and it can be a tool to further personal development.

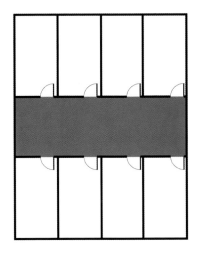
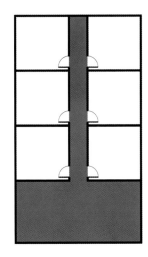
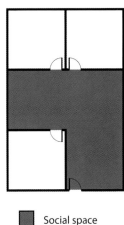

■ Social space

□ Individual space

Optional common spaces on a typical floor

In addition to supporting students' personal development, a residence can be used to promote educational programs. Innovative technologies can be included in sustainable buildings to create better living conditions and be used as a teaching tool (ETS 2012). Students may learn to live more sustainably and broaden their awareness to new advances. Moreover, the building can take on an interactive educational role and be used for research (ETS 2012).

Study spaces can serve an imperative function in the residence's educational role. It may help to define study areas that are technically distinct from entertainment areas, and also to provide a variety of individual and group spaces. These spaces should include access to necessary learning tools. Building the infrastructure that will promote and sustain the use of technology within these learning spaces is imperative for students' education. To further promote a seamless academic experience, some schools choose to include classrooms in their residences (Peterkin 2013, Concordia University n.d.).

By introducing proper design, student residences can be made to complement the overall educational experience.

Student housing also plays a role in attracting students to a particular school. A factor to consider is how the housing integrates technology, both in its marketing and within student life. Nowadays, because information is accessed online, reaching out to potential students using this medium can be beneficial and exemplifies a progressive attitude. Schools can post virtual tours or walk-throughs of their residences, along with interviews and testimonials from current users, to give potential students a realistic sense of their environment (McGill University n.d., Concordia University n.d.). The architecture of student housing should relate to the students, the surrounding city and the rest of the campus. Its design can surpass its functional role to represent students' youthful exuberance. This can be conveyed aesthetically through the use of colors and shapes in the design. Depending on the location, the building should relate to its surrounding environment as well.

The urban design of student housing within cities can be integrated into the city's fabric, so that students feel they are part of the larger urban community. It is expected that students will venture out of their residences and experience the cities in which they live. The design can welcome this exploration by incorporating itself into the city's existing environment—making use of public spaces, transportation, services and cultural locations. If there is an existing campus, designers may choose to reflect aspects of established campus buildings to represent a cohesive school environment, or they may choose to differentiate new buildings from older ones to distinguish upgrades.

Student housing has evolved to become more than mere shelters—to play an active role in the quality of education provided by schools. The projects that follow will exemplify the wide range of spaces that are provided to cater to every need students may have. They can provide privacy while encouraging socialization, study spaces and entertainment.

# Simmons Hall

**Steven Holl Architects** // Massachusetts Institute of Technology, Cambridge, United States

The Massachusetts Institute of Technology asked Steven Holl Architects to design new student housing that would foster interactions between students. The firm designed a 10-story building that acts as a "slice of the city" within the building. The building not only offers 350 dormitories, but also includes a 125-seat theater, a café/bar, and a street-level dining area, within an area of 195,000 square feet (18,116 square meters).

The structure has a gridded façade that is broken up by large openings, which work like sponges. The openings let in natural light and allow air to circulate. These openings are also used as interactive spaces for students and allow views of the surroundings. The building has a total of five openings, which are used as the main entrances, view corridors, and outdoor terraces.

The interior atrium space contrasts with the linearity of the exterior. Large organic shapes surround the staircase and sitting spaces. Social interaction is also encouraged in the interior, with the wide 11-foot (3-meter) corridor offering a space for students to meet and communicate. Each student room contains nine operable windows and a 18-inches-deep (46-centimeter-deep) wall, which permits winter sun to warm the room and, in summer, keeps the room cool. At night, some of the numerous windows light up giving a rhythmic look to the building, resembling a city skyline. Simmons Hall was successfully designed to promote student interactions and, as a result, the building is vibrant and lively.

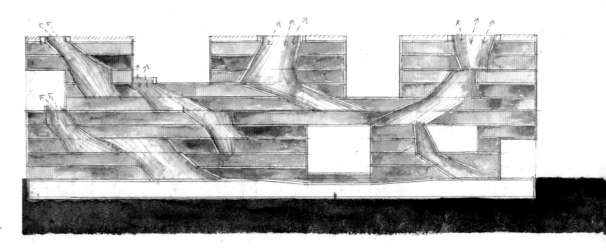

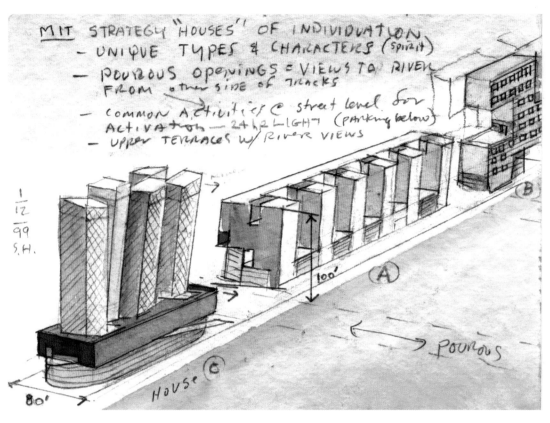

MIT STRATEGY "HOUSES" OF INDIVIDUATION
- UNIQUE TYPES & CHARACTERS (spirit)
- POUROUS OPENINGS = VIEWS TO RIVER
  FROM other side of Tracks
- COMMON Activities @ street level for
  ACTIVATION — 24h2 LIGHT (Parking below)
- UPPER TERRACES w/ River VIEWS

1/12/99 S.H.

100'

80'

HOUSE C

A

B

POUROUS

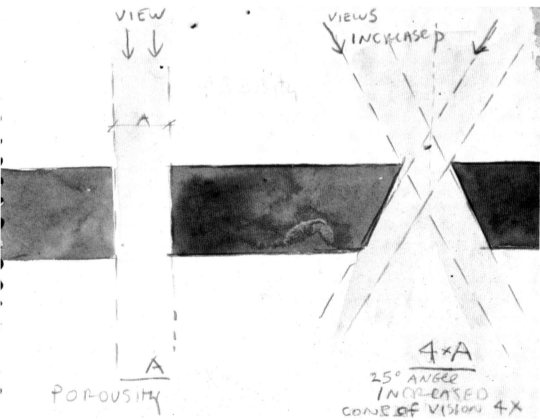

VIEW

VIEWS
INCREASED

A

A

POROUSITY

4×A
25° ANGER
INCREASED
CONE OF VISION 4X

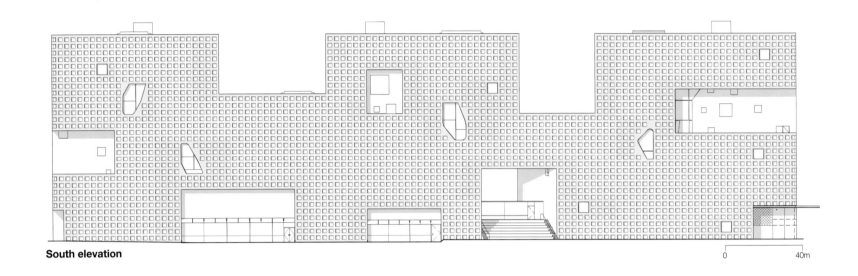

**South elevation**

0            40m

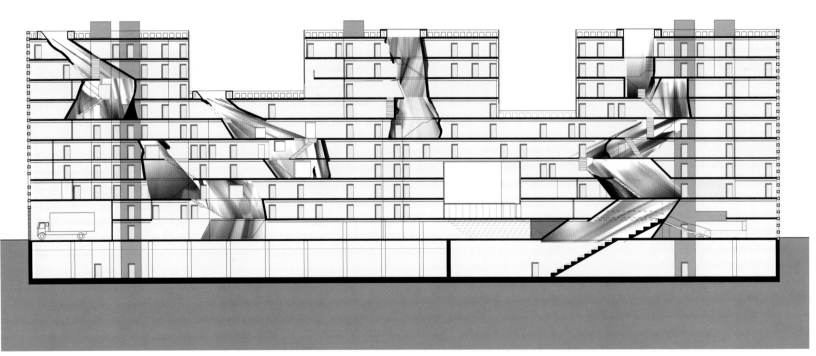

**Section**

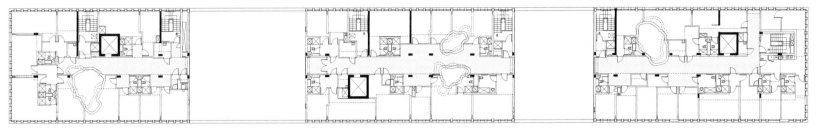

**Level 10**

**Level 5**

**Level 2**

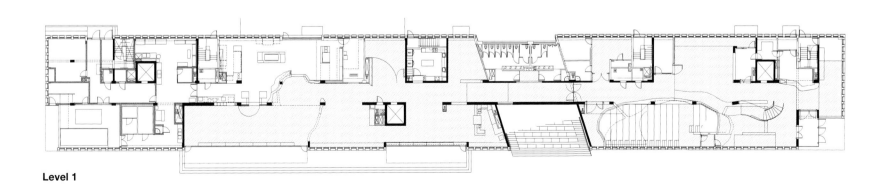

**Level 1**

# Willow Street Residence

**Mack Scogin Merrill Elam Architects** // Tulane University, New Orleans, United States

The Willow Street Residence is designed to house 330 students and includes a residential hall with a café, classrooms, and gathering spaces. Located on an urban site and streetcar route, the four buildings are a combination of solids and voids, on an area of 108,000 square feet (10,030 square meters).

The buildings are a juxtaposition of traditional New Orleans architecture with modern innovations. Transparent boxes appear to sit on large brick frames, while exterior stairs and balconies allow access to each box. Tall windows with interior wood shutters, brick and stucco façades, metalwork details, stairs, balconies, and large exterior courtyards are a few examples of New Orleans typical architecture used in the Willow Street Residence.

The large courtyards, a key design feature, include areas for interaction between students, as well as shade and vegetation. Since Willow Street Residence is located on the edge of a suburban area, respecting the privacy of the nearby homeowners was a necessity. To overcome this constraint, a garden wall was installed to screen the Audubon neighbors from the student housing. The residence offers a private sanctuary within New Orleans, allowing students to benefit from both campus and city life.

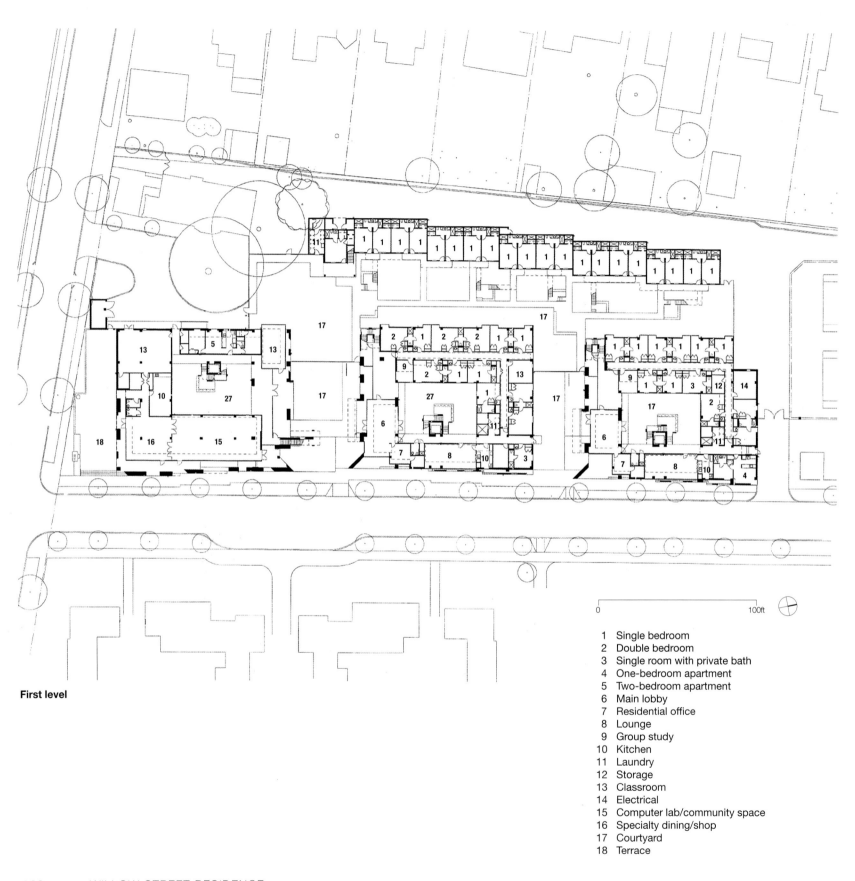

1   Single bedroom
2   Double bedroom
3   Single room with private bath
4   One-bedroom apartment
5   Two-bedroom apartment
6   Main lobby
7   Residential office
8   Lounge
9   Group study
10  Kitchen
11  Laundry
12  Storage
13  Classroom
14  Electrical
15  Computer lab/community space
16  Specialty dining/shop
17  Courtyard
18  Terrace

**First level**

0                            100ft

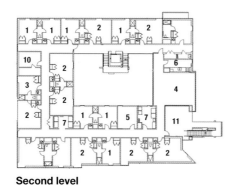

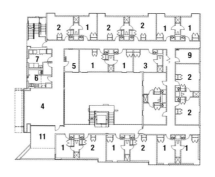

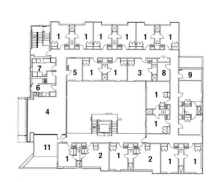

**Second level**

0        100ft

1   Single bedroom
2   Double bedroom
3   Single room with private bath
4   Lounge
5   Group study
6   Kitchen
7   Laundry
8   Storage
9   Electrical
10   Mechanical
11   Terrace

# Bikuben Student Residence

**AART architects** // University of Copenhagen, Copenhagen, Denmark

The designers of the project attempted to rethink the social environment of student life in residences and establish a community rather than just a residency. The designers set an objective to create a space that would foster interactions and avoid the lack of social relationships that are common in student residences. To maximize opportunities for personal interaction, and acquire more knowledge about social architecture, AART architects worked with anthropology students from the University of Copenhagen while designing this project. The six-story-tall building houses 107 studio apartments, a gym, terraces, party rooms and common kitchens, within an area of 75,347 square feet (7000 square meters).

The residence is shaped like a cube, with an intruded "S" of balconies dividing up the façade. The balconies are connected and continue on every face of the building.

The entrance of the building is exaggerated by the elevation of the cube, to create a welcoming open atrium. Indoors, there are two spirals surrounding the atrium. These spirals connect the residences to the common space. The meeting opportunities between students are maximized and, at the same time, the intimacy and students' privacy are not compromised.

The kitchens, living areas, gym, laundry facilities, and roof garden are staggered at different levels. The kitchens and common areas are all oriented toward the central atrium, reinforcing the idea of a social building. The architects recognized the importance of a sustainable design by using local materials. The project was also made cost effective by using prefabricated components for the façade and the bathroom elements. Bikuben Student Residence offers students a stimulating living space, within a building that promotes community.

**Level 3**

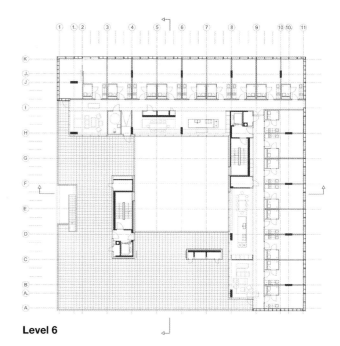

**Level 6**

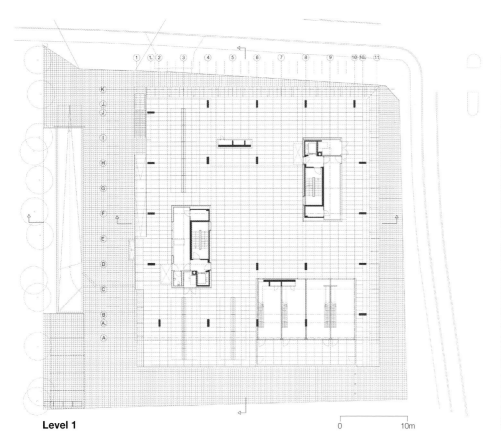

**Level 1**

0        10m

# MySpace Student Housing

**MEK architects** // University of Trondheim, Trondheim, Norway

MySpace Student Housing was built for the University of Trondheim, also known as the Norwegian University of Science and Technology, which required a student residence that would promote unity and interaction between its occupants. MEK architects innovatively approached the concept of encouraging communication. For instance, the 116 students living in the residence can enjoy the kitchen space simultaneously, an unusual format for a communal and condensed space.

The building itself detaches from its surroundings. The shape was designed to maximize views and natural light. Since it is located on the edge of Elgesetergate, which is a main road, no bedroom windows open onto that elevation. As a result, only corridors and the lounge have views of the road. The façade is clad with pine and painted in shades of gray and black.

The ground floor contains a lounge divided into smaller spaces where students meet. The bedrooms are located on the perimeters of the lounge and on the four floors above. Study areas are placed off the corridors and on the terraces to facilitate group study sessions. With the design of this residence, MEK architects highlighted the importance of social, economic and environmental innovations by developing a new type of student living, which is attractive and simple.

Level 2

Level 5

Level 1

Levels 3 and 4

0    5m

# CampagnePlein Dormitory

**Arons en Gelauff Architecten** // University of Twente, Enschede, the Netherlands

The University of Twente's nine-story-tall student residence borders a sports field and incorporates sport into its architecture. The façade facing the sports field is fitted with a 98-foot (30-meter) climbing wall. The residence is surrounded by wooded areas and was built on a former parking lot. The building, which has 152 studios, is linked to a one-story supermarket and other commercial spaces. There is also an additional row of studios on top of the lower building whose roof serves as a common garden.

The façade is made of red glass panels and dark bricks, similar to the other student residences in the university. Seen from the sports field, the dormitory appears to be "bending." A climbing wall is made of 2500 grips and is the second highest in the Netherlands. It was a gift from a visitor to the campus—the university has an active mountaineering club. The climbing wall adds an aspect of fun to the building and the campus, and stands out in contrast to the red glass façade. The western wall of the lower building is also covered in grips and can be used for climbing.

The interior courtyard of the building echoes the informality of the exterior. The studios are accessed from the courtyard, and bridges link galleries. Picnic tables, concrete stools, and bike racks are also scattered inside. The design of CampagnePlein illustrates that architecture can be playful and that such playfulness enhances student life.

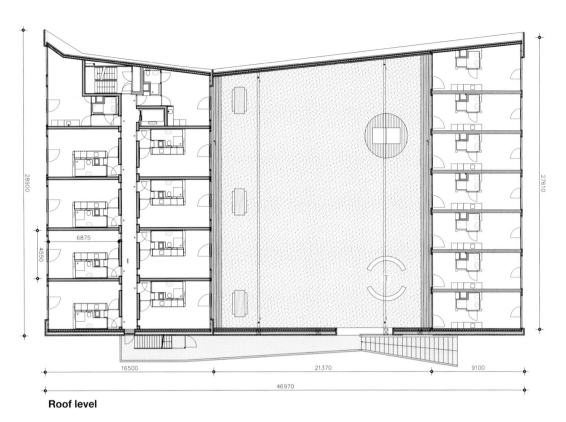

**Roof level**

28900  6875  4550  27610  16500  21370  9100  46970

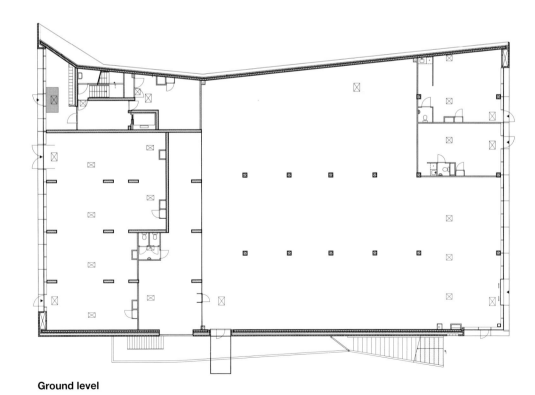

**Ground level**

# University of New South Wales Village

**Architectus** // University of New South Wales, Kensington, Australia

The award-winning University of New South Wales (UNSW) Village is one of the largest student housing complexes in Australia. Located on campus, along High Street in Sydney, it provides 240 self-contained units, with a total of 1021 rooms. The residence occupies an area of 344,445 square feet (32,000 square meters).

The Village is made up of wings that are eight stories tall, while wood panels, white and gray concrete balconies, and black accented windows mark the façades. The designers also decided to preserve the existing university buildings such as the Old Tote Theatre, the White House, and old fig trees, a heritage feature that is present throughout the entire site. The project is not only a well-functioning building—it also enhances student life through quality facilities, well-arranged common areas and energy-efficient devices. For instance, cross ventilation, generous levels of natural lighting, solar hot water systems, greywater recycling in laundries, stormwater retention and sun-shaded windows are some of the sustainable features integrated through the design.

The project promotes a friendly village atmosphere by offering community spaces and a program that focuses on supporting residents, both academically and socially. The village also explores interactive technologies. Prior to construction, future residents could appreciate the design with virtual tours of 3D-illustrated floor plans and social media campaigns. Following completion of the building, social interactions, easy communication and transfer of information were promoted with an online social media network offered by the school. UNSW Village achieved a 100 percent occupancy rate in its first year of operation, which is a telling mark of its success.

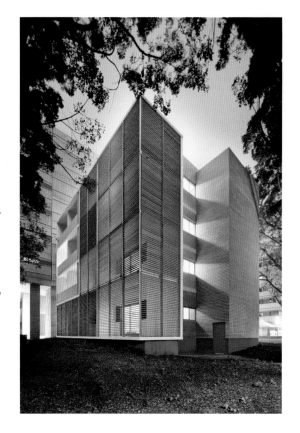

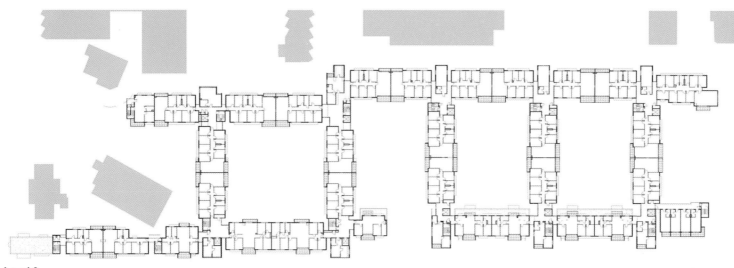

**Level 3**

# Résidences Étudiantes

**Régis Côté et associés, architectes** // École de Technologie Supérieure, Montréal, Canada

This new student residence, for the École de Technologie Supérieure in the city of Montréal, addresses environmental challenges in an innovative way. During the project's conception, priority was given to the university's sustainable policies in the design of the 287 student accommodations. As a result, energy-efficient technologies and practices were introduced throughout the 182,986-square-foot (17,000-square-meter) building.

The façade is made of prefabricated concrete panels that were produced by a local company. Horizontal and vertical windows create variation in an otherwise repetitive façade. The use of prefabrication accelerated the construction process, saving time and money. A bridge links the residences to the new pavilions of the university and a supermarket. This aerial connection made it possible to avoid the introduction of certain amenities such as the laundry room, reception, underground parking and gardens in the new building. Utility conduits were also added to the bridge to link the ventilation system to the geothermal heating source. The ventilation system recycles the heated air, and a heat pump preheats the water for domestic use.

Students can live alone or as a couple in the fully furnished apartments, which are between 387 and 581 square feet (36 and 54 square meters). Gathering and meeting places for students, such as a large interior courtyard, and various recreational common places have also been provided. This new student residence has, in itself, become a kind of laboratory and teaching instrument by incorporating innovative sustainable systems.

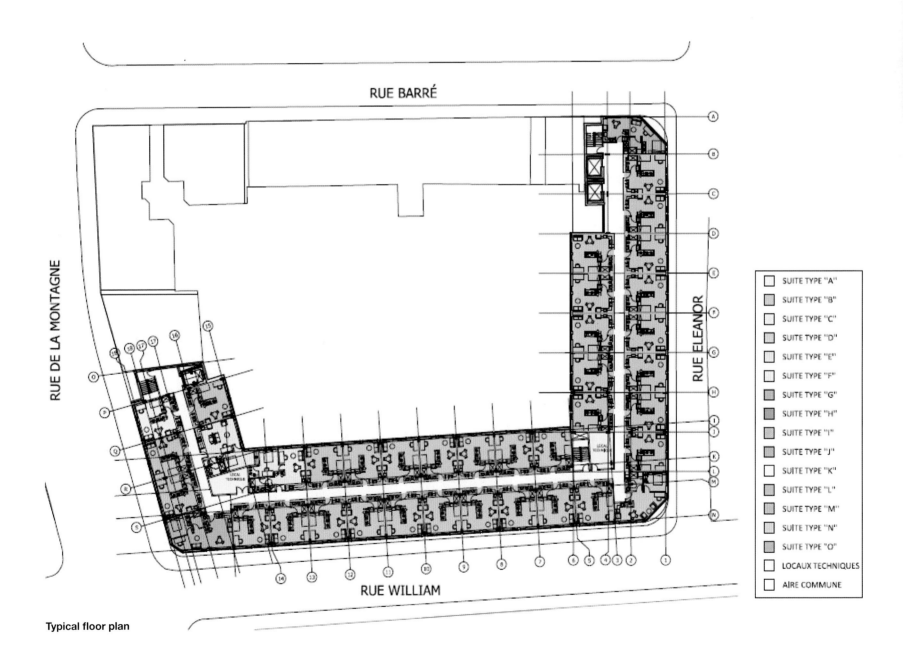

RUE BARRÉ

RUE DE LA MONTAGNE

RUE ELEANOR

RUE WILLIAM

| | SUITE TYPE "A" |
| | SUITE TYPE "B" |
| | SUITE TYPE "C" |
| | SUITE TYPE "D" |
| | SUITE TYPE "E" |
| | SUITE TYPE "F" |
| | SUITE TYPE "G" |
| | SUITE TYPE "H" |
| | SUITE TYPE "I" |
| | SUITE TYPE "J" |
| | SUITE TYPE "K" |
| | SUITE TYPE "L" |
| | SUITE TYPE "M" |
| | SUITE TYPE "N" |
| | SUITE TYPE "O" |
| | LOCAUX TECHNIQUES |
| | AIRE COMMUNE |

Typical floor plan

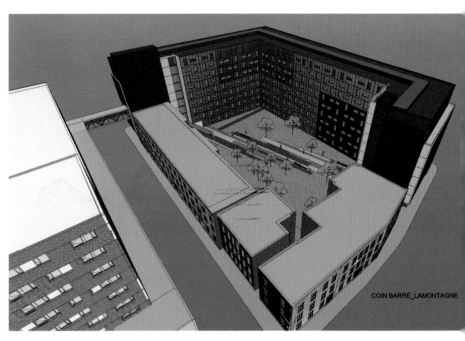

COIN BARRÉ_LAMONTAGNE

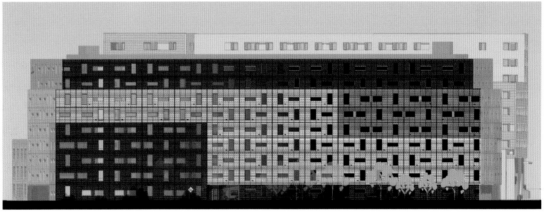

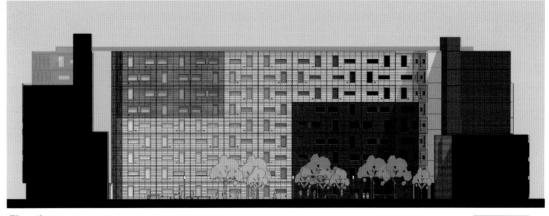

**Elevations**

0          10m

# 06 Historical Chronology

Student housing has progressed along with the evolution of education itself. The main catalysts for change in student accommodation have been societal circumstances. These have affected the roles of students and education in different nations and the way in which institutions regard their students. In fact, today, most factors evident in student housing are the direct result of student involvement in the education system since the 1960s—an era that changed the way student welfare was considered. This chapter offers a brief history of student housing in the Western world to examine how its architecture has changed and developed.

The origination of formal secular educational institutions occurred in early medieval Europe. Prior to this, education was controlled by the church. Many institutions that became universities existed long before such a title was even recognized. Gradually, schools emerged under a secular clergy as new definitions developed for what are now known as *universities* (Rait 1918). Gaining respect among wealthy patrons, these institutions attracted donations, which propagated the development of schools throughout Europe. The first official university was the University of

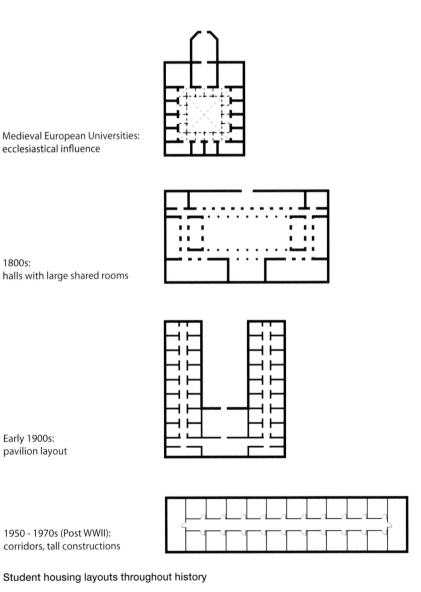

Medieval European Universities:
ecclesiastical influence

1800s:
halls with large shared rooms

Early 1900s:
pavilion layout

1950 - 1970s (Post WWII):
corridors, tall constructions

**Student housing layouts throughout history**

Bologna, established in 1088 (Scholnick 2013). Other early universities were formed in Paris and England (Rait 1918). Oxford has existed since 1096, but rapidly grew through the early 12th century (Oxford University n.d.). Cambridge was formed in the early 13th century (University of Cambridge n.d.). By the 14th century, universities were growing in popularity throughout Europe, due to donations and encouragement by royalty and the church (Rait 1918).

The student experience varied within each city and from school to school. However, into the 14th century, clearer trends and influences appeared in France, England and Italy (Rait 1918).

The first universities were conceptualized as societies rather than as physical spaces. It was not considered necessary to build housing for students (Rait 1918). A democratic system, originating in Paris but later found in most schools, emerged in the early university years, in which students lived freely in private homes and elected (among themselves) a responsible leader, who would enforce their chosen rules and manage their rent and other needs (Rait 1918). This system evolved into much stricter regulations. For example, in Oxford, it began with a benefactor, in 1270, who donated property to students. The initiator later implemented strict codes of conduct, influenced by the Mendicant and Monastic Orders, who first provided housing for their members (Rait 1918). The housing was modeled on monasteries and could include chapels, halls, libraries, even gardens and cloisters (Rait 1918). This system was adopted by both Oxford and Cambridge (Rait 1918), and would later become the model for American schools. This set a new precedent in university life, with a complex hierarchy established to enforce rigid regulations within the housing provided.

This standard remained in England; however, continental Europe and Scotland had not yet provided living arrangements in their universities (Gaines 1991). Students in Paris, Italy and Germany continued to find their own housing (Gaines 1991). This was a fundamental divide in the perceived role of the university. The English system attempted to control the entire life of the student, while in what would emerge as the German system, the university's focus was on research and teaching with little influence on the private life of the student (Frederiksen 1993).

Shortly after the foundation of the colonies in the United States, universities were established there under the influence of the English system. Harvard led the way in 1636, with other prominent schools like Yale, Princeton and Brown following in the 18th century (Scholnick 2013, Frederiksen 1993). As many of the founding leaders were Oxford and Cambridge graduates, it is clear why they chose to model their new institutions on the English system (Frederiksen 1993). In medieval Europe, when a strict system of rules and surveillance was established, students were typically 14- or 15-year-old youths entering university (Rait 1918). Similarly, in the new colonies of the United States, students were young and traveled long distances to attend the sparsely available schools (Frederiksen 1993). Therefore, the strict English *in loco parentis* (in place of parents) system was appropriately enforced. Additionally, housing was in short supply in New England, unable to sustain large amounts of students in small college towns (Frederiksen 1993).

Residences were built for the new schools– taking influence directly from England. These structures were introverted buildings with large exterior walls, separating students from the outside (Stephey n.d.). The Harvard residences

were built in quadrangular form with windows and openings only on the yard side, showing a wall to the outside; an allusion to the English colonial *yard* (Stephey n.d., Gaines 1991). These residences were mostly attended by the upper echelons of society and, as a result, the interiors had lavish public spaces, and houses were often named after distinguished families (Gaines 1991).

The first half of the 19th century saw many student rebellions and conflicts with university administrations. During the mid-19th century, many educators traveled to Germany and returned to propagate the belief that institutions should not provide housing (Frederiksen 1993). This resulted in a decline in the popularity of student residences from the 1860s until the early 20th century (Frederiksen 1993). Student housing was seen as a misuse of funds and as an influence on youth delinquency. The mindset of educators shifted from the traditional view that students needed constant supervision, to the belief that students should be left to mature independently. Consequently, the numerous universities in the United States that opened during this time excluded residence buildings in their construction, causing students to crowd into private homes within college towns (Frederiksen 1993).

Since students were left to their own devices, they formed their own communities, which led to the North American tradition of fraternities and sororities—living together in homes. Students became interested in the communities formed and the extracurricular activities that ensued (Frederiksen 1993). Student interest in academic life increased by the turn of the 20th century and schools took notice. During this time, women's colleges emerged and offered residence-based education. These new colleges, along with students' interest in

Medieval European Universities:

1800s:

Early 1900s:

1950s–1970s (Post WWII):

2000–present:

**Typical student room arrangements throughout history**

their educational communities and activities and the poor living conditions in college towns, led to a renewed interest in student residences in the United States (Frederiksen 1993).

From the Second World War onwards, student housing trends diversified around the world, varying from school to school. In Canada, for instance, the English housing system was not as influential. There were few universities that attempted to provide housing for a large number of students; most in the east were influenced by the Scottish regime of rented rooms in private homes (Klein 1969).

Variety in global trends also resulted from different approaches by governments and their divergent laws. In the United States, government land grants allowed for the development of residences on campuses at the beginning of the 20th century (Frederiksen 1993). Generally, however, the Great Depression of the 1930s, followed by the Second World War, caused a dramatic decrease in student housing construction. The large-scale nature of the war would later cause more global movements in the field of students' accommodations.

Student housing was greatly affected by the Second World War—university enrollments dropped dramatically as many young men were drafted. This left room for higher attendance rates for women and also left most dorms unused. After the war, the return of soldiers meant a large influx of students in universities and a desperate housing situation. In pre-war North America, the average citizen did not attend college. The GI Bill was passed after the war provided education for millions of veterans. In 1947, 49 percent of United States college admissions were veterans, and by the end of the original Bill in 1956, 7.8 million of the 16 million war veterans were educated (U.S. Department of Veterans Affairs 2013). The veteran presence in universities meant that most of the students were already mature adults; therefore the tradition of *in loco parentis* was no longer necessary in North American and British schools, and the role of schools in the lives of students was called into question (Klein and Sears 1969). The immediate need for housing in the post-war years led to the use of makeshift temporary housing, campers, trailers, even barracks, to house students (Frederiksen 1993, Klein and Sears 1969). A permanent, fast solution was necessary.

Soon after the war, many new dormitories were erected. There was little consideration for the quality of student life; rather low-maintenance dorms were built for maximum use in a minimum amount of space (Educational Facilities Laboratories 1972, Frederiksen 1993). New technologies, such as steel frame and prefabricated concrete panel construction, helped build the first high-rise dorms (Ingersoll and Kostof 2013). These were monolithic, monotonous, inflexible and impersonal structures that comprised of long corridors— lined with double-occupancy rooms, ending in shared bathrooms, and usually included mass dining halls and lounges (Educational Facilities Laboratories 1972).

In the 1960s, the rise of civil rights and an increasingly diverse student population protested against the monotony and administrative rule of these dormitories. Studies in the late 1960s expressed an unused potential of these dormitories and acknowledged that student residences could be used as a tool in education while serving social and developmental purposes (Ferguson 1969, Educational Facilities Laboratories 1972).

It became apparent that the residences were not serving students' needs (Ferguson 1969). There was a shift in attitude by school administrators as some universities began to experiment with different room layouts and diminished regulations (Ferguson 1969). By 1966, English universities, in particular, offered more variety in student accommodation, according to preferences (Ferguson 1969). Many of the buildings were still new in the 1960s and the cost to rebuild or renovate them was high. Also, many institutions were very traditional, insisting that students needed to adapt to the existing dorms rather than building dorms to suit students' needs. Therefore, changes were slow (Educational Facilities Laboratories 1972).

By the 1970s, students were so dissatisfied with the postwar dorms that it was common to have low occupancy rates, despite an increase in school enrollments. Students were choosing to live off-campus and pay high rents for often substandard apartments, rather than live in existing dorms (Educational Facilities Laboratories 1972). Students suffered in poor living conditions, schools lost revenues from empty residences and, overall, there was a decrease in school communities and resulting unity (Educational Facilities Laboratories 1972). The choices remained for schools to either rebuild, remodel, or stop providing housing altogether. Formation of student governments and activism helped to make changes to living conditions. Schools began to relax their rules and curfews. In addition, coeducational living was introduced for women and men (Educational Facilities Laboratories 1972). With goals aimed at increased privacy and flexibility in lifestyle and schedules, there were movements toward: more apartment-style rooms, clusters of rooms, less room sharing, fewer shared bathrooms, fewer dining halls and more kitchenettes (Educational Facilities Laboratories 1972, Devlin et al 2008). Those who rebuilt residences avoided the long hallways lined with rooms. These new trends proved to increase in popularity on a global scale and they would continue to become more popular into the 1980s.

In the 1980s and 90s, freedom in student living increased and the construction of traditional dorms from the 1950s continued to decline. There was an increased need for renovations and improvements, partly due to the advent of personal computers and technology in education. However, there was still a significant lack of interest in research into student housing, mainly because of reduced funding (Devlin et al 2008). As a result, any major advancements in the field were stalled until the late 1990s.

In the new millennium, the initial improvements suggested in the 1970s flourished. Many of the same concepts that were revolutionary at that time now became mainstream in schools.

Institutions changed their attitudes toward students as they continued to be attentive to their needs and desires. Globalization encouraged competitiveness among schools, as did student expectations for services and lifestyle. New technologies became available to lengthen the lifespan of buildings, making them energy-efficient, sustainable and easier to construct. Better survey methods were available to determine requirements and students' reactions to their living spaces.

The main goal for schools today is to satisfy its students by providing both a home and a fulfilling school experience. If students are content, the school will be successful and continue to attract the best students. With so many options available, schools can design

their housing to be unique and to represent the identity they want to portray, as well as the type of students they wish to attract. These options are available because of the long evolution of student housing—from being essential to dispensable; from undergoing strict rule to fostering independence; from segregation to inclusion. Finally, today's hope is to achieve a balance that creates the best possible home for students.

# List of Architects

**2A Design (formerly CG Architectes)**
25 ave du Général de Gaulle, F-35131
    Chartres de Bretagne, France
www.cgarchitectes.fr
infos@cgarchitectes.fr
+33 (0)2 23 25 05 76

**AART architects**
Aaboulevarden 22, 5th floor DK-8000
Aarhus C, Denmark
www.aart.dk
aart@aart.dk
+45 87 30 32 86

**Architectenbureau Marlies Rohmer**
Postbus 2835, 1000 CX Amsterdam, the
    Netherlands
www.rohmer.nl
info@rohmer.nl
+31 20 4190086

**Architectus**
Australia
Level 3, 341 George St, Sydney NSW,
    Australia 2000
www.architectus.com.au
sydney@architectus.com.au
+61 2 8252 8400

New Zealand
Level 2, 3-13 Shortland St, Auckland,
    New Zealand 1010
www.architectus.com.au
auckland@architectus.co.nz
+64 9 307 5970

**ARKITEMA Architects**
Aarhus
Frederiksgade 32, 8000 Aarhus C, Denmark
arh@arkitema.dk

København
Rued Langgaards Vej 8, 2300 København S,
    Denmark
kbh@arkitema.dk
www.arkitema.dk
+45 7011 7011

**Arons en Gelauff Architecten**
Gedempt Hamerkanaal 92, 1021 KR,
    Amsterdam, the Netherlands
www.aronsengelauff.nl
+31 (0)20 423 55 30
mail@aronsengelauff.nl

**be baumschlager eberle**
LochauLindauer Straße 31, Lochau, Austria
    6911
www.baumschlager-eberle.com
office@be-lochau.com
+43 5574 43079-0

**Bevk Perović Arhitekti**
Dunajska 49, SI-1000 Ljubljana, Slovenia
www.bevkperovic.com
info@bevkperovic.com
+386 1 241 76 30

**bogevischs buero**
Architekten & Atadtplaner gmbh,
    Schulstraße 5 80634, Munich, Germany
www.bogevisch.de
buero@bogevisch.de
+46 89 452 35 47 0

**Carrier Johnson + Culture**
1301 Third Ave, San Diego, CA, United States
    92101
http://www.carrierjohnson.com/
https://smtp.carrierjohnson.com/owa
+1 619 239 2353

**Charlotte Cattani and Alberto Cattani
Architectes**
6 Rue Gobert 75011 Paris, France
http://alberto-cattani-architecte.blogspot.ca
01 43 70 10 39

**dataAE**
Bailèn 28, 2on 1a. Barcelona, Spain
www.dataae.com
dataAE@dataAE.com
0034 93 265 19 47

**Emmanuel Combarel Dominic Marrec
Architectes**
7, passage Turquetil 75011, Paris, France
www.ecdm.eu
ecdm@ecdm.fr
+33 1 44 93 20 60

**Fact Architects**
Weesperzijde 111 K, 1091 EN, Amsterdam,
    the Netherlands
www.factarchitects.nl
mail@factarchitects.nl
+31 20 4633793

**GWP Architecture**
Bracken Housing, 1 Lidgett Ln, Leeds,
    United Kingdom LS8 1PQ
http://gwp-arch.com
architecture@gwp-arch.com
0113 266 6044

**H Arquitectes**
Carrer de Montserrat, 22, 2n, 2a, 08201,
    Sabadell, Spain
www.harquitectes.com
harquitectes@harquitectes.com
0034 93 725 00 48

**Hawkins\Brown**
159 St John St, London, United Kingdom
    EC1V 4QJ
www.hawkinsbrown.com
mail@hawkinsbrown.com
020 7336 8030

**Haworth Tompkins Architects**
33 Greenwood Pl, London, United Kingdom
    NW5 1LB
www.haworthtompkins.com
info@haworthtompkins.com
+44 020 7250 3225

**JAHN (formerly Murphy/Jahn)**
35 East Wacker Dr, Suite 300, Chicago, IL,
    United States 60601
http://www.jahn-us.com
info@jahn-us.com
+1 312 427 7300

**KieranTimberlake**
420 North 20th St, Philadelphia, PA,
    United States 19130-3828
www.kierantimberlake.com
academic@kierantimberlake.com
+1 215 922 6600

**Lundgaard & Tranberg Arkitekter**
Pilestræde 10, 3. Sal, 1112 København K,
    Denmark
www.ltarkitekter.dk
mail@ltarkitekter.dk
+45 33 91 07 17

**Mack Scogin Merrill Elam Architects**
111 John Wesley Dobbs Ave, NE Atlanta, GA,
    United States 30303
www.msmearch.com
office@msmearch.com
+1 404 525 6869

**Mahlum**
71 Columbia, Floor 4, Seattle, WA, United States
    98104
www.mahlum.com
info@mahlum.com
(206) 441-4151

**Mateo Arquitectura**
Teodor Roviralta 3908022, Barcelona, Spain
www.mateo-arquitectura.com
info@mateo-arquitectura.com
+34 932 186 358

**Mecanoo Architecten**
Oude Delft 203, 2611 HD Delft, the
    Netherlands
www.mecanoo.nl
info@mecanoo.nl
+31 15 2798100

**MEK architects**
Julianalaan 2A, 2628 BH Delft, the Netherlands
www.mek-architects.com
info@mek-architects.com

**NOBEL arkitekter**
Vestergade 11, 1456 København K, Denmark
www.nobel.dk
nobel@nobel.dk
+45 33 18 11 30

**OFIS Arhitekti**
Tavcarjeva 2, 1000 Ljubljana, SI, Slovenia
www.ofis-a.si
project@ofis.si
+386 1 4260084

**Régis Côté et associés, architectes**
111 rue Abraham-Martin, bureau 500,
    Québec, Canada G1K 8N1
www.regiscote.com
Info_qc@regiscote.com
+1 418 692 4617

**Silvester Fuller**
Studio 502 19A Boundary St, Rushcutter Bay,
    NSW, Australia 2011
www.silvesterfuller.com
mail@silvesterfuller.com
+61 (0)2 9360 1122

**Steven Holl Architects**
450 West 31st St, 11th floor, New York, NY,
    10001, United States
www.stevenholl.com
nyc@stevenholl.com
+1 212 629 7262

**Studio E Architects**
2258 First Ave, San Diego, CA, United States
    92101
www.studioearchitects.com
info@studioearchitects.com
619 235 9262

**Studioninedots (formerly HVDN
Architecten)**
Gedempt Hamerkanaal 111,
1021 KP, Amsterdam, Netherlands
http://www.studioninedots.nl
info@studioninedots.nl
+31 204889269

**Tempohousing Global**
H.J.E. Wenckebachweg 49aNL-1096 AK,
    Amsterdam, the Netherlands
www.tempohousing.com
info@tempohousing.com
+31 20 468 33 93

**Tétreault Parent Languedoc &
Saia Barbarese Topouzanov**
5605 Ave de Gaspé, Suite 504, Montreal,
    Canada
www.sbt.qc.ca
msaia@sbt.qc.ca
514 866 2085

**Tony Owen Partners**
Level 2, 12-16, Queen St
Chippendale, NSW, Australia 2008
www.tonyowen.com.au
info@tonyowen.com.au
+61 2 96982900

**Werner Wirsing**
No contact details available.

# Bibliography for Chapters

Abel, Jaison R., and Richard Deitz (February 13, 2012). "How Colleges and Universities Can Help Their Local Economies" in *Liberty Street Economics*, accessed May 7, 2014 from http://libertystreeteconomics.newyorkfed.org

Abraham, Sabrina (January 7, 2014). "University Requests Proposals for Housing Expansion Project" in *University of Ottawa Gazette*, accessed May 19, 2014 from http://www.gazette.uottawa.ca/en/2014/01/university-requests-proposals-for-housing-expansion-project/

Anchors, Scott, and Roger B. Winston Jr. "Student Development in the Residential Environment" in *Student Housing and Residential Life*, edited by Ursula Delworth, Jossey-Bass Inc., San Francisco, 1993, pp. 25–64.

Anchors, Scott, Katie Branch Douglas and Mary Kay Kasper. "Developing and Enhancing Student Communities" in *Student Housing and Residential Life*, edited by Ursula Delworth, Jossey-Bass Inc., San Francisco, 1993, pp. 461-480.

Beddoes, David W., and Colin A. Booth. "Insights and Perceptions of Sustainable Design and Construction" in *Solutions to Climate Change Challenges in the Built Environment*, edited by Colin A. Booth, Felix N. Hammond, Jessica E. Lamond and David G. Proverbs, Blackwell Publishing Ltd., 2012, pp. 127-140, accessed April 30, 2014 from DOI: 10.1002/9781444354539.index..

Blimling, Gregory S. "New Challenges and Goals for Residential Life Programs" in *Student Housing and Residential Life*, edited by Ursula Delworth, Jossey-Bass Inc., San Francisco, 1993, pp. 1–20.

BREEAM. "What is BREEAM" accessed July 10, 2014 from http://www.breeam.org/about.jsp?id=66

CalRecycle [last updated March 5, 2012]. "Green Building Materials" accessed July 10, 2014 from http://www.calrecycle.ca.gov/greenbuilding/materials/

Canadian Architect (November 7, 2013). "Forum York Development Corporation and York University to Implement New Student Housing and Mixed-Use Project" accessed May 19, 2014 from http://www.canadianarchitect.com/news/forum-york-development-corporation-and-york-university-to-implement-new-student-housing-and-mixed/

Cardenas, Alberto, and Fernando Domenech (2005). "Assembly Required" in *American School & University*: 78.4. *Global Reference on the Environment, Energy, and Natural Resources*, accessed April 30, 2014 from http://find.galegroup.com.proxy1.library.mcgill.ca/grnr/infomark.do

Chiarantoni, Carla. "La Residenza Temporanea per Studenti", Alinea, Florence, 2008.

Common Ground (2013). "Cost-Efficient Housing Models" accessed May 13, 2014 from http://commongroundwa.org/organization/NHMI-cost-effficient-models

Concordia University. "Residence Life" accessed May 28, 2014 from http://www.concordia.ca/campus-life/residences.html

Cost of Solar. "15 Solar Energy Facts (That You Should Know)" accessed July 10, 2014 from http://costofsolar.com/15-solar-energy-facts-that-you-should-know/

Devlin, Ann Sloan, Sarah Donovan, Arianne Nicolov, Olivia Nold, and Gabrielle Zandan (2008). "Residence Hall Architecture and Sense of Community: Everything Old is New Again" in *Environment and Behavior*, 40:487, accessed June 12, 2014, from DOI: 10.1177/0013916507301128.index.

Educational Facilities Laboratories. *Student Housing*, New York, 1972.

Ekundayo, Damilola, Srinath Perera, Chika Udeaja, and Lei Zhou. "Achieving Economic and Environmental Sustainability Through Optimum Balance of Costs." Proceedings of the 10th International Postgraduate Research Conference, University of Salford, United Kingdom, 14–15 September 2011, pp. 673-684, accessed June 25, 2014 from http://www.academia.edu/901071/Achieving_economic_and_environmental_sustainability_through_optimum_balance_of_costs

ETS. "286 Nouveaux Appartements Pour Les Etudiants." Nov 23, 2012, accessed May 30, 2014 from http://www.etsmtl.ca/nouvelles/2012/Nouvel-ilot-de-residences

Ferguson, D.S. *Student Housing Report*, Ontario Department of University Affairs, Toronto, 1969.

Ferrante, Julia (August 3, 2010). "'Green Roof' Will Serve as Learning Lab, Demo For Future" in *Bucknell University*, accessed July 10, 2014 from http://www.bucknell.edu/x63562.xml

Fisher, Karin (August 23, 2012). "International Admission Offers Continue to Grow at U.S. Graduate Schools, Mostly Because of China" in *The Chronicle of Higher Education*, accessed May 7, 2014 from https://chronicle.com/article/International-Admissions/133910

Frederiksen, Charles F. "A Brief History of Collegiate Housing" in *Student Housing and Residential Life: A Handbook for Professionals Committed to Student Development Goals*, edited by Ursula Delworth, Jossey-Bass Inc., San Francisco, 1993, pp. 167-184.

Friedman, Avi. *Fundamentals of Sustainable Dwellings*, Island Press, Washington, 2012.

Friedman, Avi. *Innovative Housing: Concepts for Sustainable Living*, Laurence King Publishing Ltd., London, 2013.

Friedman, Avi. *The Adaptable House: Designing Homes for Change*, McGraw-Hill, New York, 2002.

Gaines, Thomas A. *The Campus as a Work of Art*, Praeger, Westport, CT, 1991.

Galindo, Michelle, and Martin Nicholas Kunz, (eds). *Best Designed Modular Houses*, AV edition, Stuttgart, 2005.

Gittleman, Mara. "Green Roof FAQs". *Tufts University Office of Sustainability*, accessed July 10, 2014 from http://sustainability.tufts.edu/green-roof-collaborative/

Goldbaum, Ellen (May 13, 2009). "Solar Energy to Power Student Apartments" in *University at Buffalo Reporter*, accessed July 10, 2014 from http://www.buffalo.edu/ubreporter/archive/2009_05_13/solar_array

Greentechmedica. "U.S. Solar Market Insight Report" accessed July 10, 2014, http://www.greentechmedia.com/research/ussmi

Greenwashing Index. "Greenwashing Index" promoted by EnviroMedia Social Marketing and the University of Oregon, accessed July 10, 2014 from http://www.greenwashingindex.com/about-greenwashing/

Hardiman, Tom (December 1, 2011). "Piece by Piece in School Construction" in *American School & University* [Online Exclusive] *Global Reference on the Environment, Energy, and Natural Resources*, accessed April 30, 2014 from http://find.galegroup.com.proxy1.library.mcgill.ca/grnr/infomark.do

Harvard University. "Harvard University Housing" accessed May 19, 2014 from http://www.huhousing.harvard.edu/

Holmes, Selina (May 5, 2014) "Top 10 Countries for LEED" in USGBC accessed July 10, 2014 from http://www.usgbc.org/articles/top-10-countries-leed

Ingersoll, Richard, and Spiro Kostof. *World Architecture: A Cross-Cultural History*, Oxford University Press, New York, 2013.

International Energy Agency. "Sustainable Buildings" accessed April 30, 2014 from http://www.iea.org/topics/sustainablebuildings

JISC (Higher Education Funding Council for England [HEFCE] 2006), "Designing Spaces for Effective Learning: A Guide to 21st Century Learning Space Design" accessed May 13, 2014 from http://www.jisc.ac.uk/uploaded_documents/JISClearningspaces.pdf

Johnson, Ingrid, Michael Leachman, Phil Oliff, and Vincent Palacios (March 19, 2013). "Recent Deep State Higher Education Cuts May Harm Students and the Economy for Years to Come" in *Center on Budget and Policy Priorities*, accessed May 7, 2014 from http://www.cbpp.org/cms/

Kennet, Miriam. "Green Economics Dialogue and the Built Environment" in *Solutions to Climate Change Challenges in the Built Environment*, edited by Colin A. Booth, Felix N. Hammond, Jessica E. Lamond and David G. Proverbs, Blackwell Publishing Ltd., 2012, pp. 57–74, accessed April 30, 2014 from DOI: 10.1002/9781444354539.index.

Klein, Jack, and Henry Sears. *Habitat de l'étudiant: étude sur le logement des étudiants*, Association des Universitiés et Collèges du Canada, Ottawa, 1969.

Lacey, Stephen (December 17, 2013). "The Most Important Solar Statistics of 2013" in *Greentechmedia*, accessed July 10, 2014 from http://www.greentechmedia.com/articles/read/the-most-important-solar-statistics-of-2013

Li, Hao (April 21, 2011). "Why Racial Quotas in University Admissions Are Unfair." *International Business Times*, accessed May 5, 2014 from http://www.ibtimes.com/why-racial-quotas-university-admissions-are-unfair-280875

Macintyre, Clement (2003). "New Models of Student Housing and Their Impact on Local Communities" in *Journal of Higher Education Policy and Management*, 25:2. pp.109-18, accessed May 5, 2014. DOI: 10.1080/1360080032000122598.index.

Magar, Christine S.E. "Seven Principles for Interconnectivity: Achieving Sustainability in Design and Construction" in *Sustainable Communities Design Handbook*, edited by Woodrow W. Clark II, Butterworth-Heinemann, Burlington, MA, 2010, pp. 165–79, accessed June 25, 2014 from http://www.sciencedirect.com.proxy2.library.mcgill.ca/science/book/9781856178044

McGill University. "Downtown Undergraduate Residences" accessed May 19, 2014 from http://www.mcgill.ca/students/housing/prospective/downtown-undergrad

Metcalf, Taylor (August 7, 2011). "Recycling + Building Materials" in *ArchDaily*, accessed July 10, 2014 from http://www.archdaily.com/?p=155549

Mostaedi, Arian. *Great Spaces: Flexible Homes*. Links, Barcelona, 2006.

Mullins, William, and Phyllis Allen. *Student Housing: Architectural and Social Aspects*, Crosby Lockwood, London, 1971.

OECD. "Tertiary level educational attainment for age group 25–64" in *Education: Key Tables* from OECD. No. 4. 2009. DOI: 10.1787/20755120-2009-table3.index.

Oxford University. "Introduction and History" accessed June 15, 2014 from http://www.ox.ac.uk/about/organisation/history

Palmer, Alasdair (April 21, 2012). "Setting Quotas for Universities Would Spell Academic Ruin" in *The Telegraph,* accessed May 5, 2014 from http://www.telegraph.co.uk/education/universityeducation/9218080/Setting-quotas-for-universities-would-spell-academic-ruin.html

Peterkin, Caitlin (2013). "Colleges Design New Housing as an Experience to Engage and Retain Students" in *The Chronicle of Higher Education*, 59.20. *Global Reference on the Environment, Energy, and Natural Resources,* accessed April 30, 2014 from http://find.galegroup.com.proxy1.library.mcgill.ca/

Pidou, Marc, Fayyaz Ali Memon, Tom Stephenson, Bruce Jefferson, and Paul Jeffrey (2007). "Greywater Recycling: Treatment Options and Applications" in *Engineering Sustainability* 160 ES3 ( pp. 119-31, accessed July 10, 2014 from DOI: 10.1680/ensu.2007.160.3.119.index.

Porterfield, William D., and David B. White. "Psychosocial Development in College" in *Student Housing and Residential Life*, edited by Ursula Delworth, Jossey-Bass Inc., San Francisco, 1993, pp. 65-94.

Rait, Robert S. *Life in the Medieval University*. Cambridge University Press, 1918, accessed June 15, 2014 from http://www.gutenberg.org/files/20958/20958-h/20958-h.htm

Sassi, Paola. *Strategies for Sustainable Architecture*, Taylor & Francis, New York, 2006.

Schneider, Tatjana, and Jeremy Till. *Flexible Housing*. Elsevier B.V., Oxford, 2007.

Scholnick, Dorothy. "The History of Student Housing Facilities," accessed June 12, 2014 from http://prezi.com/scg46fnxd1eb/the-history-of-student-housing-facilities/

Shimm, Jon (2001). "Sustainable Campus Housing" in *American School & University* 73.12: 142, *Global Reference on the Environment, Energy, and Natural Resources*, accessed April 30, 2014 from http://find.galegroup.com.proxy1.library.mcgill.ca/

Stephey, M.J. "The Evolution of the College Dorm" in *TIME*, accessed June 12, 2014 from http://content.time.com/time/photogallery/0,29307,1838306,00.html

Susman, Anna (June 21, 2012). "Dorm Room Evolution: What's Next?" in *Huffington Post*, accessed June 12, 2014 from http://www.huffingtonpost.com/2012/06/20/the-evolution-of-the-dormroom_n_1613037.html

Taylor, Anne P., and Katherine Enggass. *Linking Architecture and Education: Sustainable Design for Learning Environments*, University of New Mexico Press, Albuquerque, 2009, accessed June 25, 2014 from http://muse.jhu.edu.proxy2.library.mcgill.ca/books/9780826334091

United Nations Economic Commission for Europe. *Conference of European Statisticians Recommendations on Measuring Sustainable Development*, United Nations, New York, 2014, accessed July 2, 2014 from http://www.unece.org/fileadmin/DAM/stats/publications/2013/CES_SD_web.pdf

University of British Columbia. "Student Housing" accessed May 28, 2014 from http://www.housing.ubc.ca/application-info-okan/integrated-learning-communities

University of Cambridge. "Early Records" accessed June 15, 2014 from http://www.cam.ac.uk/about-the-university/history/early-records

University of Chicago. "Campus North Residence Hall and Dining Commons" accessed May 28, 2014 from http://housing.uchicago.edu/houses_houses/campus_north_residence_hall_and_dining_commons/

University of Idaho. "Green Roof Project" accessed July 10, 2014 from http://www.uidaho.edu/studentaffairs/idaho-commons-and-student-union/student-union/about-the-sub/green-roof-project

University of Oregon. "University Housing" accessed May 28, 2014 from http://housing.uoregon.edu/about/missionstatement.php.

University of Tennessee December 11, 2013). "UT Announces Student-Focused Housing Redevelopment Plan" accessed May 19, 2014 from http://tntoday.utk.edu/2013/12/11/ut-announces-student-focused-housing-redevelopment-plan/

University of Toronto. "Student Housing and Residence Life" accessed May 28, 2014 from http://www.utm.utoronto.ca/housing/students-families/residence-life

U.S. Department of Veterans Affairs [last updated November 21, 2013]. "Education and Training," accessed June 15, 2014 from http://www.benefits.va.gov/gibill/history.asp

The U.S. Environmental Protection Agency [last updated July 9, 2012], "An Introduction to Indoor Air Quality (IAQ)" accessed July 10, 2014 from http://www.epa.gov/iaq/voc.html

U.S. Green Building Council (USGBC). "About USGBC" accessed July 10, 2014 from http://www.usgbc.org/About

U.S. Green Building Council (USGBC) "LEED" accessed July 10, 2014 from http://www.usgbc.org/leed

Van Mourik, Jaime (June 7, 2012). "Fostering a Generation of Sustainability Natives" in U.S. Green Building Council (USGBC), accessed July 2, 2014 from  http://www.usgbc.org/articles/fostering-generation-sustainability-natives

Vinnitskaya, Irina (March 17, 2012). "UC Davis West Village/ Studio E Architects" in *ArchDaily*, accessed April 30, 2014 from http://www.archdaily.com/215764/uc-davis-west-village-studio-e-architects/

Williams, Daniel E. *Sustainable Design: Ecology, Architecture, and Planning*. Wiley, Hoboken, NJ, 2007.

Wilson, Jen (May 18, 2012). "Campus Crest to add solar panels for student housing" in *Charlotte Business Journal*, accessed July 10, 2014 from http://www.bizjournals.com/charlotte/news/2012/05/18/campus-crest-solar-city-to-install.html

Wines, James. *Green Architecture*, edited by Philip Jodidio. Taschen, Los Angeles, 2000.

Zadeh, Sara, Rachel Lombardi, Dexter Hunt, and Christopher Rogers (November 30, 2012). "Greywater Recycling Systems in Urban Mixed-Use Regeneration Areas: Economic Analysis and Water Saving Potential" in *2nd World Sustainability Forum*, accessed July 10, 2014 from www.sciforum.net/conference/wsf2/paper/1021/download/pdf

Zaransky, Michael H. Profit By Investing in *Student Housing: Cash in on the Campus Housing Shortage*. Dearborn Trade, Chicago, 2006, http://site.ebrary.com.proxy1.library.mcgill.ca/lib/mcgill/docDetail.action?docID=10118540

# Bibliography for Projects

## 1.1 West Campus Student Housing Phase I
ArchDaily. "West Campus Student Housing/Mahlum" accessed July 31, 2013 from http://www.archdaily.com/408376/west-campus-student-housing-mahlum-architects/

## 1.2 West Village (first phase)
ArchDaily. "UC Davis West Village/Studio E Architects" accessed May 25, 2013 from http://www.archdaily.com/215764/uc-davis-west-village-studio-e-architects/
UC Davis. "UC Davis West Village Backgrounder" accessed April 28, 2014 from http://westvillage.ucdavis.edu/press-kit/backgrounder.html

## 1.3 Smarties, Uithof
ArchDaily. "380 Student Units and Public Space Design/Architectenbureau Marlies Rohmer" accessed May 10, 2013 from www.archdaily.com/120265/380-student-units-and-public-space-design-architectenbureau-marlies-rohmer/
Architectenbureau Marlies Rohmer. "Smarties, Uithof" accessed May 10, 2013 from www.rohmer.nl/?view=detail&pageAlias=projecten&subAlias=highlights&naamLetter=&jaarId=&werkveldId=&stadLetter=&landId=&projId=22
Architizer. "Smarties, Uithof" accessed May 10, 2013 from www.architizer.com/en_us/projects/view/smarties-uithof/20679/#.UYz9FHDA5UQ

## 1.4 Student Village
ArchDaily. "Student Village/Hawkins\Brown" accessed May 9, 2013 from www.archdaily.com/219713/student-village-hawkinsbrown/
Campbell-Dollaghan, Kelsey. "Elegant Student Housing, for Future Veterinarians On-Call at All Hours" accessed May 9, 2013 from www.fastcodesign.com/1670480/elegant-student-housing-for-future-veterinarians-on-call-at-all-hours#6
Hawkins\Brown. "Royal Veterinary College" accessed May 9, 2013 from www.hawkinsbrown.com/projects/royal-veterinary-college

## 1.5 Student Apartments in the Olympic Village
Bogevischs Buero. "Remodelling of 1052 student apartments in the Olympic Village, Munich" accessed May 8, 2013 from www.bogevisch.de/en/projects/082.html
Detail Inspiration. "Renewal of the Student Apartments at the Olympic Village in Munich" accessed May 8, 2013 from http://detail-online.com/inspiration/renewal-of-the-student-apartments-at-the-olympic-village-in-munich-103535.html
Paul, Jochen. "Profile Bogevischs Buero" accessed May 8, 2013 from www.baunetz.de/talk/crystal/pdf/en/talk6.pdf

Paul, Jochen. "Stylish Living in the Smallest Spaces—New Design for Student Housing" accessed April 30, 2014 from www.goethe.de/kue/arc/nba/en10037405.htm

## 1.6 Newington Green Student Housing
Haworth Tompkins. "Newington Green" accessed May 8, 2013 from www.haworthtompkins.com/built/proj19/index.html
Mozas, Javier. Dbook: Density, Data, Diagrams, Dwellings: a Visual Analysis of 65 Collective Housing Projects. a+t Ediciones, Vitoria, 2007.
Sanctuary Students. "Alliance House, Newington Green" accessed May 1, 2014 from www.haworthtompkins.com/built/proj19/index.html

## 1.7 Student Housing Duwo
e-architect. "Student Housing Delft" accessed May 3, 2013 from www.e-architect.co.uk/holland/delft_student_housing.htm

## 2.1 Zuiderzeeweg
ArchDaily. "Zuiderzeeweg/Fact Architects" accessed May 9, 2013 from www.archdaily.com/118318/zuiderzeeweg-fact-architects/
Meinhold, Bridgette. "Zuiderzeeweg: Modular Student Housing can be Moved to Another Location" accessed May 9, 2013 from http://inhabitat.com/zuiderzeeweg-modular-student-housing-block-can-be-moved-to-a-new-location/

## 2.2 Student Housing
ArchDaily. "Student Housing (Universitat Politècnica de Catalunya)/H Arquitectes + dataAE" accessed May 3, 2013 from www.archdaily.com/327868/student-housing-universitat-politecnica-de-catalunya-h-arquitectes-dataae/
Dezeen. "Student Housing in St. Cugat by H Arquitectes and dataAE", accessed May 3, 2013 from www.dezeen.com/2013/02/05/student-housing-in-st-cugat-by-h-arquitectes-and-dataae/

## 2.3 Keetwonen (Amsterdam Student Housing)
Open Architecture Network. "Keetwonen (Amsterdam Student Housing)" accessed May 28, 2013 from http://openarchitecturenetwork.org/projects/6354

## 2.4 Signalhuset
ArchDaily. "Signalhuset/NOBEL" accessed May 24, 2013 from www.archdaily.com/1416/signalhuset-nobel/

## 2.5 La Résidence Pour Étudiants du Havre en Containers Maritimes

Alberto Cattani Architecte. "La Résidence pour Étudiants du Havre en Containers Maritimes" accessed May 3, 2013 from http://alberto-cattani-architecte.blogspot.ca/2010/10/residence-pour-etudiants-le-havre.html

Contemporist. "Cité A Docks Student Housing by Cattani Architects" accessed May 3, 2013 from www.contemporist.com/2010/09/30/cite-a-docks-student-housing-by-cattani-architects/

## 2.6 Qubic

HVDN Architecten. "Qubic" accessed May 3, 2013 from www.hvdn.nl/2111/projecten/0342ste.htm

Walsh, David. "Dutch Architects Reinvent Modular Construction" accessed May 1, 2014 from www.djc.com/news/ae/12011276.html

## 3.1 Tietgen Dormitory

Cotter, Molly. "Copenhagen's Tietgenkollegiet Dorm is the Coolest Circular Housing Complex on Campus" accessed May 6, 2013 from http://inhabitat.com/lundgaard-and-tranbergs-tietgenkollegiet-dorm-is-the-coolest-circular-housing-on-campus/

Lundgaard & Tranberg Arkitekter. "Tietgen Dormitory" accessed May 6, 2013 from www.ltarkitekter.dk/en/projects/5

## 3.2 Champion Hill Residences

www.kcl.ac.uk/campuslife/accom/kings/kingsresidences/championhill.aspx

## 3.3 State Street Village

Architizer. "State Street Village" accessed May 26, 2013 from www.architizer.com/en_us/projects/view/state-street-village/4184/#.UaJe_JVM7ww

Chicago magazine. "State Street Village (2003)" accessed May 26, 2013 fromwww.chicagomag.com/Chicago-Magazine/September-2007/Ten-Modern-Masterpieces/The-List/index.php

Mi Modern Architecture. "State Street Village" accessed May 26, 2013 from www.mimoa.eu/projects/United%20States/Chicago/State%20Street%20Village

## 3.4 Languedoc

Architecture Lab. "Languedoc, Rennes/France by CGArchitectes" accessed May 2, 2014 from http://architecturelab.net/2010/12/languedoc-france-by-cgarchitectes/

Poireau, Kévin. "Résidence Étudiante Languedoc à Rennes par CG Architectes" accessed May 17, 2013 from http://www.actuarchi.com/2011/02/residence-etudiante-languedoc-rennes-cg-architectes/

## 3.5 Basket Apartments

ArchDaily. "Basket Apartments in Paris / OFIS Architects" accessed May 2, 2013 from http://www.archdaily.com/280195/basket-apartments-in-paris-ofis-architects/

e-architect. "Paris Student Apartments" accessed May 5, 2014 from www.e-architect.co.uk/paris/paris-student-studios

OFIS. "Paris Student Apartments" accessed May 3, 2013 from www.ofis-a.si/str_9%20-%20housing/7_paris_student_apartments/ofis_paris_student_apartments.html

## 3.6 UQAM Campus

ArchDaily. "UQAM's Campus/Tétreault Parent Languedoc + Saia Barbarese Topouzanov" accessed July 29, 2015 from http://www.archdaily.com/9986/uqams-campus-tetreault-parent-languedoc-saia- barbarese-topouzanov/

## 3.7 Te Puni Village

ArchDaily. "Te Puni Village/Architectus" accessed May 25, 2013 from www.archdaily.com/140692/te-puni-village-architectus/

Hawkins Construction. "Te Puni Village" accessed May 5, 2014 from http://hawkinsconstruction.co.nz/te-puni-village/

## 3.8 Student Housing Poljane

Afasi. "Bevk Perovic Arhitekti" accessed May 5, 2013 from http://afasiaarq.blogspot.com/2012/07/bevk-perovic-arhitekti.html

Mi Modern Architecture. "Student Housing Poljane" accessed May 5, 2013 from http://mimoa.eu/projects/Slovenia/Ljubljana/Student%20Housing%20Poljane

## 3.9 Colegio Mayor Sant Jordi

Arqua. "Colegio Mayor Sant Jordi en Barcelona" accessed May 6, 2013  from http://arqa.com/arquitectura/internacional/colegio-mayor-sant-jordi-en-barcelona.html

Language International. "International House Barcelona" accessed May 6, 2014 from www.languageinternational.ca/school/international-house-barcelona-62875/housing

Mi Modern Architecture. "Colegio Mayor Sant Jordi" accessed May 6, 2013 from http://www.mimoa.eu/projects/Spain/Barcelona/Colegio%20Mayor%20Sant%20Jordi

## 3.10 Résidence Étudiante et Résidence Médicalisée

Dezeen. "Residence à Epinay sur Seine by ECDM" accessed May 5, 2013 from www.dezeen.com/2009/07/10/residence-a-epinay-sur-seine-by-ecdm/

ECDM. "Résidence étudiante et résidence médicalisée—Epinay-sur-Seine" accessed May 5, 2013 from http://ecdm.eu/?p=117

Mi Modern Architecture. "Student Housing in Epinay" accessed May 5, 2013 from www.mimoa.eu/projects/France/Epinay%20sur%20Seine/student%20housing%20in%20Epinay

Plus Mood. "Résidence étudiante & médicalisée | ECDM" accessed November 25, 2014 from https://web.archive.org/web/20131127105433/http://plusmood.com/2010/01/the-residence-etudiante-medicalisee-ecdm

## 3.11 Ernie Davis Hall

AIA Georgia. "People's Choice Award Submission: Ernie Davis Hall" accessed August 12, 2015 from https://www.aiaga.org/design_awards/ernie-davis-hall/

Syracuse University. "Facility Information: Ernie Davis Hall" accessed August 12, 2015 from http://housingmealplans.syr.edu/facilityinformation_erniedavis.cfm

## 4.1 Sustainable Student Residences

Jones, Will. "Top marks for university eco-residences" accessed May 15, 2014 from www.building.co.uk/top-marks-for-university-eco-residences/3115378.article

GWP Architecture. "Lancaster University Student Housing" accessed May 15,
2014 from http://gwp-arch.com/projects/lancaster-university-cg/
UPP. "Lancaster University" accessed May 15, 2014 From www.upp-ltd.com/
lancaster-university.php

**4.2 The Residential Life Project**
Carrier Johnson + CULTURE. "Pitzer College Residential Life" accessed May 7,
2014 from www.carrierjohnson.com/projects/education/view/29/pitzer-
college-residential-life
PCL Construction. "Pitzer College Student Housing Phase 2" accessed May 21,
2013 from www.pcl.com/Projects-that-Inspire/Pages/Pitzer-College-Student-
Housing-Phase-2.aspx
Pitzer College. "Pitzer Goes Platinum: The Residential Life Project" accessed
May 22, 2013 from www.pitzer.edu/sustainability/rlp.asp
Pitzer College. "Residential Life" accessed May 22, 2013 from www.pitzer.edu/
student_life/residence_life/housing.asp

**4.3 Ungdomsboliger Aarhus Havn**
Arkitema Architects. "Ungdomsboligerne—Aarhus Harbour" accessed May
6, 2013 from www.stateofgreen.com/en/Profiles/Arkitema-K-S/Solutions/
Ungdomsboligerne---Aarhus-harbour
Boligforeningen Ringgården."Sustainable Student Housing Aarhus Harbour"
accessed May 8, 2014 from www.bf-ringgaarden.dk/media/77149/symbook.pdf
Mi Modern Architecture. "Ungdomsboliger Aarhus Havn" accessed May 6,
2013 from www.mimoa.eu/projects/Denmark/Aarhus/Ungdomsboliger%20
Aarhus%20Havn

**4.4 Student Guest House**
ROCKWOOL. "Oead-Gästehaus Molkereistrasse" accessed May 7, 2013 from
www.rockwool.es/obras+de+referencia/u/2011.case/2068/New+build/
OeAD-Gästehaus+Molkereistrasse?lang=es

**4.5 Charles David Keeling Apartments**
American Institute of Architects. "Charles David Keeling Apartments" accessed
May 13, 2013 from www.aiatopten.org/node/79
KieranTimberlake. "Keeling Apartments" accessed May 13, 2013 from
www.kierantimberlake.com/pages/view/21/charles-david-keeling-apartments/
parent:3

**4.6 Boston University Sydney Academic Centre**
ArchDaily. "New Student Quarters For Boston University/Tony Owen Partners &
Silvester Fuller" accessed May 14, 2013 from www.archdaily.com/110896/
new-student-quarters-for-boston-university-tony-owen-partners-silvester-
fuller-architects/
Arthitectural. "Tony Owen Partners | Boston University Student Housing"
accessed May 14, 2013 from www.arthitectural.com/tony-owen-partners-
boston-university-student-housing/

**5.1 Simmons Hall**
ArchDaily. "Simmons Hall at MIT/Steven Holl" accessed May 25, 2013 from
www.archdaily.com/65172/simmons-hall-at-mit-steven-holl/
Stevel Holl Architects. "Simmons Hall, Massachusetts Institute of Technology"
accessed May 25, 2013 from www.stevenholl.com/project-detail

**5.2 Willow Street Residence**
Architecture Week. "South Atlantic AIA Design Awards" accessed May 26, 2013
from www.architectureweek.com/2003/1112/news_1-1.html
Mack Scogin Merrill Elam Architects. "Tulane University—Willow Street
Residence Hall" accessed May 26, 2013 from msmearch.com/type/
academic/tulane-university-willow-street-residence-hall

**5.3 Bikuben Student Residence**
AART Architects. "Bikuben Dormitory" accessed May 12, 2014 from aart.dk/
projects#_node-200
World Buildings Directory. "Bikuben Student Residence" accessed May 6, 2013
from www.worldbuildingsdirectory.com/project.cfm?id=832

**5.4 MySpace Student Housing**
ArchDaily. "Trondheim Student Housing / MEK Architects" accessed May 16,
2013. from www.archdaily.com/284331/trondheim-student-housing-mek-
architects/
Dezeen. "MySpace student housing in Trondheim by MEK Architects" accessed
May 16, 2013 from www.dezeen.com/2012/11/10/myspace-student-
housing-in-trondheim-by-murado-elvira-krahe-architects/

**5.5 CampagnePlein Dormitory**
ArchDaily. "University of Twente Campus buildings / Arons en Gelauff
Architecten" accessed May 12, 2014 from www.archdaily.com/21556/
university-of-twente-campus-buildings-arons-en-gelauff-architecten/
Arons en Gelauff. "Climb Your Dorm" accessed May 3, 2013 from
http://aronsengelauff.nl/housing/105
Contemporist. "New Student Housing at the University of Twente" accessed
May 3, 2013 from www.contemporist.com/2008/12/23/new-student-
housing-at-the-university-of-twente/

**5.6 University of New South Wales Village**
Architectus. "UNSW Village" accessed May 12, 2014 from www.architectus.
co.nz/en/projects/unsw-village#
Campus Living Villages. "UNSW Village" accessed May 26, 2013 from
www.campuslivingvillages.com/Australia/About-Us/case-studies/UNSW-
Village-case-study.html
UNSW Village. "UNSW student village awarded for architectural excellence"
accessed May 26, 2013 from www.unswvillage.com.au/lifestyle/news/
UNSW-student-village-awarded-for-architectural-excellence.html

**5.7 Résidences Étudiantes**
ÉTS. "New Units Available on Campus" accessed May 13, 2014 from
http://en.etsmtl.ca/en/Student-Information/Housing/Phase-4
ÉTS. "Nouvel îlot de residences" accessed May 15, 2013 from
www.etsmtl.ca/nouvelles/2012/Nouvel-ilot-de-residences

# Photography Credits

All photography is copyright © and reprinted courtesy of those listed below.

**1.1 West Campus Student Housing Phase I**
Benjamin Benschnieder

**1.2 West Village (first phase)**
JBL Photography (page 18), Fred Larson Photography (page 20) and Jeff Peters Photography (pages 19, 21)

**1.3 Smarties, Uithof**
AkzoNobel (page 27, top left), Scagliola en Brakkee (pages 26; 27, top right, center right and bottom left) and Rene de Wit (page 23)

**1.4 Student Village**
Tim Crocker

**1.5 Student Apartments in the Olympic Village**
bogevischs buero

**1.6 Newington Green Student Housing**
Morley Von Sternberg (page 35, 36; bottom left), Philip Vile (pages 34, 36; right, 37) and Lukasz Kowalski (page 36; top left)

**1.7 Student Housing Duwo**
Exterior photography by Christian Richters
Interior photography by Mateo Arquitectura

**2.1 Zuiderzeeweg**
Luuk Kramer

**2.2 Student Housing**
Adrià Goula

**2.3 Keetwonen (Amsterdam Student Housing)**
Tempo Housing

**2.4 Signalhuset**
Jens Lindhe (pages 60, 61, 62, 63; bottom right) and NOBEL arkitekter (page 63; bottom left, top right)

**2.5 La Résidence Pour Étudiants du Havre en Containers Maritimes**
Charlotte Cattani and Alberto Cattani Architectes and Vincent Fillon

**2.6 Qubic**
Luuk Kramer

**3.1 Tietgen Dormitory**
Jens Lindhe (pages 77, 78) and Lundgaard & Tranberg Architects (page 79)

**3.2 Champion Hill Residences**
James Mumby (pages 83, 84, 85) and John Wybor (page 81)

**3.3 State Street Village**
Doug Snower (page 89; left, top right, bottom right) and Rainer Viertlboeck (pages 86, 87, 88)

**3.4 Languedoc**
2A Design

**3.5 Basket Apartments**
Tomaz Gregoric

**3.6 UQAM Campus**
Marc Cramer (page 102; top) Alain Laforest (pages 100, 101, 102; bottom, 103; left) and Vladimir Topouzanov (page 103; top right and bottom right)

**3.7 Te Puni Village**
Paul McCredie

**3.8 Student Housing Poljane**
Miran Kambic

**3.9 Colegio Mayor Sant Jordi**
Beat Marugg

**3.10 Résidence Étudiante et Résidence Médicalisée**
Benoît Fougeirol

**3.11 Ernie Davis Hall**
Timothy Hursley (pages 120; top and bottom, 124; top, bottom right, 125; top left, bottom right), Maren Guse (pages 124; bottom left, 125; top right) and Sterling Surfaces (pages 121, 122)

**4.1 Sustainable Student Residences**
Martine Hamilton-Knight Photography

**4.2 The Residential Life Project**
Costea Photography

**4.3 Ungdomsboliger Aarhus Havn**
Arkitema Architects

**4.4 Student Guest House**
Eduard Hueber/archphoto

**4.5 Charles David Keeling Apartments**
Tim Griffith

**4.6 Boston University Sydney Academic Centre**
Tony Owen Partners

**5.1 Simmons Hall**
Steven Holl Architects

**5.2 Willow Street Residence**
Timothy Hursley

**5.3 Bikuben Student Residence**
AART architects

**5.4 MySpace Student Housing**
Miguel de Guzman (pages 176, 179) and Mathias Herzog (page 177)

**5.5 CampagnePlein Dormitory**
Jeroen Musch

**5.6 University of New South Wales Village**
John Gollings

**5.7 Résidences Étudiantes**
Bernard Fougères (pages 188, 191; top left) and Serge Jacques (pages 189, 191; top right)

# Index